"Kirby Reutter delivered again! His dialectical behavioral therapy (DBT) self-help book teaches trauma survivors to go beyond numbing their pain; rather, they are guided in restoring the balance of their thoughts and emotions. Reutter breaks down 'applied mindfulness' into eye-opening sections that can speak to all. The enlightening flow from acceptance to action, accompanied by his therapeutic tools, such as the RAIN DANCE technique, will work to navigate through relationships, life, and self. His adaptation of DBT for post-traumatic stress disorder sufferers will help to facilitate healing the pain now and in the future with supportive exercises throughout this book."

> —**Iva Svancarova**, clinical mental health counselor and DBT enthusiast currently practicing in New York, NY

"Kirby Reutter has used his knowledge, passion, and experience to write a workbook that is applicable to individuals that struggle with trauma. His approach through real examples, along with his unique sense of humor, is truly captured in his work. I have worked alongside him; the workbook reads as many of his therapy sessions would play out. He uses language that is understandable and relatable, and offers a vantage point that allows individuals to feel comfortable and as though this is a journey and not a life sentence. He provides the education and tools needed, offering support throughout the process of healing."

> —**Nicole Johnson-Smith, MS, CCTP, LMHC-A**, director of the LaGrange County Northeastern Center, and adjunct faculty of the Jannen School of Arts and Sciences at Trine University

"Restoring balance! Kirby Reutter has compiled many useful exercises to aid anyone in the healing process. I have used his exercises in my own life and in my practice with counseling women who have experienced trauma, and I have recommended his work for individuals to use on their own. Reutter frames concepts in a way that is very practical and useful. These exercises are easy to use and demonstrate growth. I am excited to have this resource published and available for a wider population to access for their own healing."

> —**Charla Leman, LCSW, CADAC IV**, supervising counselor at Gateway Woods Family Services, cofounder of the drug and alcohol program at Gateway Woods Residential Services, and cofounder of BASICS at Ohio University Counseling and Psychological Services

T0301139

"Very engaging from the first page. Kirby Reutter does a great job of taking twenty years of trauma psychoeducation and breaking it down into terms that are understandable. Each chapter has a brief explanation followed by an exercise to work through. I enjoy the 'congratulations' at the end of each exercise. It makes you feel like you accomplished something. I also like the fact that you can work at your own pace and make choices about the action you will take. I feel that this is very empowering in trauma work. I cannot wait to use this with clients!"

—**Vikki Heins, MA, LMHC**, twenty years of work in the field of trauma and addictions

"Drawing from a growing body of evidence-based support for the use of dialectical behavior therapy in treating those suffering lasting effects of trauma, Kirby Reutter delivers an incredible collection of skills and exercises to help foster healing for these individuals. This workbook provides invaluable tools in an encouraging and accessible manner, while also offering honest and realistic guidance on when seeking additional professional help may be most prudent. *The Dialectical Behavior Therapy Skills Workbook for PTSD* is most assuredly a crucial, cutting-edge resource for clients as well as clinicians."

—**Sheresa Wilson-DeVries, PA-C, LMCHA**, physician assistant in the family medicine and addictions clinic at the ProMedica Coldwater Regional Hospital; and adjunct professor in the department of physician assistant studies at Trine University

"This workbook has extremely well-thought-out organization and techniques to follow, which allows those suffering from post-traumatic stress disorder (PTSD) to use this workbook for self-help or with a therapist. It is a workbook that truly guides the PTSD sufferer toward healing, rather than mainly a study guide that teaches the reader only information. These workbook exercises are clear, easy to understand, and easy to apply."

—**Harriet Farney, PhD**, education management consultant

"Having had the privilege to take one of Kirby Reutter's workshops, I was delighted to know that he had created *The Dialectical Behavior Therapy Workbook for PTSD*. What a wonderful way to explain dialectical behavior therapy in common, everyday language. This is a workbook that can be considered the light at the end of the tunnel for those suffering post-traumatic stress disorder (PTSD) as well as so many other disorders. Simple steps and amazing exercises to calm the chaos in our minds is what I found, and I include myself in dealing with my own PTSD."

—**Annemarie Maroney, AMFT**, creator of HELP from Ana Maroney

"As a US Army corpsman serving as a combat medic and a medical lab tech at the 93rd Evacuation Hospital in Long Binh, Vietnam, I was exposed to far too much human carnage, body bags, drug abuse, and waste of young lives. Then after my tour of duty, I returned home to continue what I thought was a normal life. But after I experienced these traumatic events, they just didn't go away. For over forty years, I realized that no matter what I tried, I could not just 'get over it.' At the urging of my family, and having a VA disability rating that provided mental health treatment, I sought professional help and was diagnosed with post-traumatic stress disorder (PTSD). After a few counseling visits, my journey to recovery began. Kirby Reutter's *The Dialectical Behavior Therapy Skills Workbook for PTSD* was prescribed early on in my treatment, and I could see myself over and over again. Each chapter covers a different segment of the reoccurring theme of 'restoring balance' in all aspects of life, followed by 'The Last Word,' which made it not only understandable, but also applicable. This is a very well-written workbook, and I highly recommend this workbook for any PTSD-recovering combat soldier."

—**Duane Boyd**, US Army MOS 92B10, 92B20; Vietnam veteran from 1970–1972

"Kirby Reutter presents a unique, fresh, and user-friendly perspective applying dialectical behavior therapy (DBT) concepts and skills to trauma and post-traumatic stress disorder (PTSD). His use of short, simple acronyms to remember critical concepts with clients is refreshing and most importantly useful! Clinicians want to turn to something they can use with clients NOW. Reutter provides us with that and more. He created flow and explanation in this workbook that are easy to learn and easy to teach clients. I have taught and developed DBT programs for twenty years and will be keeping this book front and center in my work!"

—**Beth Robbins, PsyD**, licensed clinical psychologist

"Kirby Reutter expertly guides the mental health practitioner and the trauma sufferer, alike, through the pursuit of balance, utilizing dialectical behavior therapy (DBT) techniques cherry-picked for their utility. Reutter patiently and effectively explains the processes with a teacher's heart, building on and reinforcing concepts previously delivered. He is a delight to learn from in person; reading his writing is the next best thing to listening to him directly! This book will be a go-to compendium many times in my work with clients!"

—**Roger Gasser, LPCC, LMHC, CADAC IV**, worked in both public and private school settings; as a faith-based counselor in a teenage residential facility, and as a therapist in a national denomination's call-in agency

"Few pastors are prepared to truly understand the impact of abuse and other forms of trauma when they begin their service—much less understand how to provide counseling support that is effective. Kirby Reutter's workbook provides structure and guidance in a form that is easy to follow. It is written in simple language that all can understand. His humor-tinged approach invites engagement and encourages follow-through each step of the way. I wish I would have had this workbook years ago!"

—**Mike Leman, LICM**, served as the overseeing pastor of churches in the United States and Mexico since 2002, providing counseling to numerous trauma survivors

"This workbook is a gift for everyone who struggles with trauma-related mental health challenges. The approach is supportive and caring. The language is easy to understand, with examples, activities, and tools that facilitate change. Although created for individuals with post-traumatic stress disorder, it can be useful for anyone that struggles with emotional or relationship issues. Kirby Reutter has developed a therapeutic approach that empowers clients to take control of their mental health, and he now shares it with us. Clinicians will find this to be an excellent adjunct to therapy, and clients will treasure it as a resource to revisit during difficult times."

—**Silvia M. Bigatti, PhD**, professor at the Richard M. Fairbanks School of Public Health at Indiana University—Purdue University Indianapolis

"Kirby Reutter does an excellent job of incorporating evidence-based concepts, practical skills, and real-life examples. Greatly simplifies the coursework, making it easy to follow for the reader. Encourages and motivates one in their journey through their own path of healing. This workbook is an excellent tool that would benefit trauma survivors and those working in the field of trauma."

—**Danette Montoya, MSW, LCSW**, psychotherapist and military sexual trauma coordinator at the San Francisco VA Health Care System

"A one-of-a-kind self-help workbook that conquers various essential aspects regarding taking control of your symptoms and getting back in the driver's seat of your life. A very thorough, straightforward, and hands-on approach to overcoming trauma and post-traumatic stress disorder. Kirby Reutter really nails the therapy toolbox. I would highly recommend this book as a complementary source to therapy, or for one who chooses to attempt to work through things on his or her own."

—**Amber Weiss, LMHC, NCC**, in private practice in Manhattan

"Kirby Reutter has created an invaluable resource for applying scientifically proven dialectical behavior therapy (DBT) skills to treat anxiety and post-traumatic stress disorder (PTSD). Written in easy-to-understand, nontechnical language, *The Dialectical Behavior Therapy Skills Workbook for PTSD* is a welcome addition to the field and will help clinicians and clients alike master the necessary skills in regulating emotions while discovering new ways to tolerate stressful situations in the context of mindfulness."

> —**Allan J. Katz, LPC/CSAT**, director of Rediscovery Counseling and Coaching in Memphis, TN; and coauthor of *Experiential Group Therapy Interventions with DBT*

"Kirby Reutter's *The Dialectical Behavioral Therapy Skills Workbook for PTSD* is an accessible, intelligently written, and hope-inspiring resource for trauma survivors and professionals working with survivors. Through encouraging exercises, memorable acronyms, supporting research, and use of humor, Reutter has crafted a workbook that provides clients the opportunity to improve their relationship to self, others, and their environment. Effectively and thoroughly described techniques help illuminate the path of healing and growth. There is a harmony between skill development and self-reflection presented, which supplies survivors with the direction needed to construct the life and change they desire."

> —**Jennifer Young, MA, LPC**, private group practice practitioner

"Kirby Reutter's workbook fills a critical need for individuals with post-traumatic stress disorder to embark on a journey toward improved emotion regulation, distress tolerance, interpersonal relationships, and self-esteem in a compassionate and validating manner. I especially appreciate the inclusion of a strong empirical foundation, in true scientist-practitioner form, that is often lacking in other self-help books. As a psychologist in independent practice for over twenty years who regularly uses dialectical behavior therapy approaches with a variety of patients, I strive to find effective, engaging, and evidence-based tools to supplement psychotherapy. With contagious enthusiasm, and the use of vivid metaphors and handy mnemonics, the author has produced a workbook that is fresh and relatable, sparks curiosity, and keeps one's interest to the very end with practical and effective exercises. I will be using this with my patients!"

> —**Cheryl L. Hall, PhD**, psychologist and past president of the Texas Psychological Association

"Kirby Reutter provides simple techniques to follow that can help many people suffering from post-traumatic stress disorder. He teaches us to be aware of our emotions and respond in a way that can be helpful for all of us, leading to better relationships and ultimately a better quality of life."

> —**Tabor Dizon, PA-C, MHS**, psychiatry and urgent care medicine

The Dialectical Behavior Therapy Skills Workbook

for

PTSD

Practical Exercises for
Overcoming Trauma &
Post-Traumatic Stress Disorder

KIRBY REUTTER, PhD

New Harbinger Publications, Inc.

Publisher's Note

This publication is designed to provide accurate and authoritative information in regard to the subject matter covered. It is sold with the understanding that the publisher is not engaged in rendering psychological, financial, legal, or other professional services. If expert assistance or counseling is needed, the services of a competent professional should be sought.

This book is independently authored and published and is not endorsed or sponsored by or affiliated with any third party. By way of example, this book is not endorsed by or affiliated in any way with Dr. Marsha M. Linehan, who is recognized as a pioneer in the field of Dialectical Behavior Therapy.

NEW HARBINGER PUBLICATIONS is a registered trademark of New Harbinger Publications, Inc.

Distributed in Canada by Raincoast Books

Copyright © 2019 by Kirby Reutter
New Harbinger Publications, Inc.
5674 Shattuck Avenue
Oakland, CA 94609
www.newharbinger.com

Automatic Negative Thoughts (ANTS) material, pages 121-122, adapted from Judith Beck (2011), *Cognitive Behavior Therapy: Basics and Beyond, Second Edition.* Used by permission of The Guilford Press.

DEAR acronym material, pages 175-177, adapted from Marsha Linehan (2015), *DBT Skills Training Manual, Second Edition.* Used by permission of The Guilford Press.

Cover design by Amy Shoup

Acquired by Jess O'Brien

Edited by Marisa Solís

All Rights Reserved

Library of Congress Cataloging-in-Publication Data on file

Book printed in the United States of America

24	23	22			
10	9	8	7	6	5

Contents

Foreword

It never fails. Whenever the topic of dialectical behavioral therapy (DBT) comes up, people have really strong feelings about it. Maybe it's all that Latin in there? I feel that DBT, for whatever reason, has been severely misunderstood and undervalued. For goodness' sake, I have worked with professionals in the field who told me that they don't bother to learn about DBT because they have no intentions of working with personality disorders!

"It's so much more!" I would argue. "You can use it for almost anything, and you should!"

Then they would inevitably look at me like I had two heads (super appropriate) and dismiss the argument. Such small-mindedness!

Well, luckily, along comes the very talented Kirby Reutter to not only herald the great value of dialectical behavioral therapy but also create a delightful workbook that applies DBT to post-traumatic stress disorder, one of our most significant and difficult-to-manage diagnoses. Here, in this informative volume, you will find all you need to quickly apply even the most complicated aspects of DBT to manage your trauma symptoms.

In my practice, I find that people are often shocked at how easily accessible DBT is. Most of the time, people are already using it and don't even know they are! When I went to my first Marsha Linehan (she's the grand dame of DBT, don't you know) training, I'll be honest: I was one of the naysayers as well. My boss was forcing me to go, and I honestly had no real interest in it: I just needed some CEUs. Then Marsha herself showed up with no shoes! She explained that she simply had forgotten to pack her shoes and decided barefoot was the way to go until she had time to manage the problem. DBT in action!

I was spellbound: Here was a practitioner who focuses on loving yourself, warts and all, practicing what she preached. Got a problem? Solve it based on what is available to you, and don't stress about what isn't or what you could have done differently. She was no nonsense, no holds barred, and I loved every minute of that training. A DBT-phile was born!

Now, I am a very eclectic therapist, and I feel that every patient is an individual who needs to be treated with respect and patience to help them find their best life. Sometimes that means introducing people to DBT. The very next time I see them, they will tell me that they Googled it (never Google mental health disorders, never!) and inevitably they ask me if I think they have a personality disorder. Sometimes they are quite offended. This is why books like the one you are holding in your hands are so important: They help break down the stigma of this unique treatment protocol so it can be expertly applied to many different disorders.

Specifically, I have used DBT with PTSD and found it to be wonderfully rewarding for my patients, and now Kirby has given me so many more new options for my therapy toolbox. Being the ninja therapist that I am means that I have to stay on my game, and having visionaries like Kirby around keeps me on my toes.

So dive right in: Poke around this beautiful tome and enjoy it like a great meal. Sample it, mull it over, doggie bag it for later. This is a book you will find yourself reaching for again and again in the future. I always tell my patients, "I don't treat broken people. I treat beautiful people who need a little polish every now and then so they can shine like they're meant to."

—Dawn DePasquale, LMHC

Losing Your Balance: The Effects of Trauma

Trauma affects different people in different ways. But there's one thing trauma always does: It throws you off balance. In fact, the effects of trauma can you leave you feeling so out of sync that you may wonder if anyone understands you—including yourself!

But you are not alone. Every year millions of people experience the effects of trauma. They feel as if their lives have been shattered. But here's the good news: Both modern science and ancient wisdom can help us not only restore our balance but also create a beautiful new mosaic out of the shattered pieces.

Trauma, by definition, is an extreme situation that forces us to react in extreme ways. Trauma drives us to respond in ways that are different from our normal way of doing things. And that's precisely why we feel so "off" during and following a traumatic event.

Sometimes the symptoms of trauma last long after the traumatic situation has ended. This is what psychologists call *post-traumatic stress disorder*—in other words, the "trauma after the trauma." This happens when the aftermath of the trauma ends up causing even more ongoing problems than the original trauma itself.

If you have been traumatized, then you know what it's like to live at the extremes, to feel out of sync with others, and even to feel at war with yourself. Sometimes you completely space on details...and sometimes you obsess over minutia. Sometimes you overreact...and sometimes you feel completely paralyzed. Sometimes you experience a million contradictory emotions at once...and sometimes you just feel numb. Sometimes you overthink with constant worries...and sometimes you make impulsive decisions by not thinking enough. Sometimes you over-rely on other people by acting too needy and clingy...and sometimes you burn bridges that you cannot afford to burn.

In short, not only do you feel like your entire life is off balance and out of whack, you also feel like a complete walking contradiction. With just about everything in your life, you experience either one extreme or the other—and sometimes both extremes at once! In fact, trauma has a way of throwing people off balance in five key areas: *awareness, reactions, emotions, thoughts,* and *relationships.* So it's no wonder that sometimes you feel "crazy."

THE THERAPEUTIC APPROACH USED IN THIS BOOK

But here's the bright side: There is an entire treatment model that is designed to restore balance in your awareness, your reactions, your emotions, your thoughts, and your relationships. The model is called *dialectical behavior therapy (DBT).* "Dialectical" is just a fancy philosophy term that means "bringing together opposites." (What a perfect concept for someone who feels like a walking contradiction!) DBT is all about finding the middle path between overreacting and underreacting, between overfeeling and underfeeling, between overthinking and underthinking, and between overreliance and underreliance on others. In short, DBT is about restoring balance to the parts of your life that trauma has forced to the extremes. In fact, if I could rename DBT using the same initials, I would probably call it *developing balance therapy!*

So how does DBT restore balance? So glad you asked! DBT works by teaching a variety of skills that will help you regain the balance that trauma has disrupted. In particular, DBT will teach you how to:

- Become more aware—and accepting—of yourself and others

- Cope better with stress and triggers

- Better regulate your thoughts and emotions

- Improve your relationships with other people

Many therapeutic models are effective in treating trauma symptoms. I chose to emphasize DBT in this workbook for several reasons:

1. DBT has been shown to be effective in treating each of the imbalance issues caused by trauma, as described above.

2. DBT is a very practical model that teaches concrete skills you can apply immediately—right here, right now.

3. All of the skills included in this workbook can be learned and practiced on your own, regardless of whether you are currently in therapy.

4. Research has found DBT to be effective with a host of other disorders closely associated with trauma, including insomnia, anxiety, attention deficit/hyperactivity disorder (ADHD), depression, oppositional defiance, various eating disorders, and borderline personality disorder.

5. DBT is very compatible with other models for treating trauma symptoms; the skills you learn in this book will only enhance the insights you can learn from other sources.

WHAT YOU WILL LEARN

The structure of this workbook is straightforward and easy to follow. It is divided into seven chapters. Each chapter is designed to restore balance in a specific area that has been affected by trauma. In addition, each chapter is subdivided into specific lessons. These lessons will teach you important skills for coping with trauma symptoms and for living a balanced, satisfying life.

In the first two chapters, you will learn how to become more aware and more accepting through a process called *mindfulness*. In the third chapter, you will learn more effective ways of coping with stress and triggers. In chapters 4 and 5, you will learn how to manage your thoughts and feelings. In the sixth chapter, you will learn how to develop healthier relationships. And in the final chapter, you will learn how to apply all of the skills you have learned in this workbook so that you can continue your journey toward health, healing, and happiness.

To be clear, working your way through this workbook will require…*work!* You will be prompted to provide lots of processing and personal reflections as you learn various skills and concepts. Some of these skills and concepts might be difficult to grasp at first—and even more difficult to *apply*.

There should be enough space in this workbook itself to jot down your initial thoughts. However, it may be a good idea to also have access to your own personal journal in case you need more space.

Because each chapter builds on themes from previous chapters, it will usually make the most sense to proceed in the order in which the chapters are presented.

To get the most out of this workbook, I recommend spending about thirty minutes a day on these exercises. I also recommend revisiting these chapters as many times as necessary for the skills and concepts to sink in. I especially recommend working through this workbook with the support of a trusted friend, pastor, rabbi, mentor, sponsor, or professional counselor. Change does not happen overnight; it may take several months of time and patience before you start to see some of your efforts pay off. Don't give up!

I hope you enjoy the journey. Let's get started!

CHAPTER 1

Restoring Balance with Mindfulness

According to the *New York Times*, a young woman learned about the horrors of severe mental illness the hard way, literally: by bashing her head against the wall of a locked cell. The young woman arrived at the Institute of Living, in Hartford, Connecticut, on March 9, 1961, at age seventeen. She was quickly admitted to the seclusion room on the unit known as Thompson Two—reserved for the most psychologically ill patients. The treatment providers had no other choice: the young woman routinely attacked herself, burning her wrists with cigarettes while slicing her arms, legs, and other body parts with any sharp object she could locate. The seclusion room—a tiny cell with a bed, a chair, and a small barred window—was strategically cleared of all such objects. And yet her urge to die only got worse.

At the facility, the doctors diagnosed the young woman with schizophrenia; prescribed Thorazine, Librium, and other potent medications; provided hours of psychoanalysis; and restrained her for electroshock treatments: fourteen shocks the first time and sixteen the second (according to her medical records). But after all that...nothing changed!

Before long, the young woman was back in seclusion and locked in her cell. Her discharge summary, dated May 31, 1963, recorded the following observations: "During 26 months of hospitalization, Miss Linehan was, for a considerable part of this time, one of the most disturbed patients in the hospital" (Carey 2011).

This young woman was Marsha Linehan, the creator of *dialectical behavior therapy*. Not only did she survive her adolescence, Linehan even made it into college, where she studied psychology. In fact, Linehan went on to earn a master's in psychology, followed by a doctorate in psychology—then she became a psychologist herself! Once Dr. Linehan was a psychologist, little by little, through lots of research and experimentation, she developed the model now called dialectical behavior therapy, or DBT for short.

WHAT IS DIALECTICAL BEHAVIOR THERAPY?

So what is DBT, and what does "dialectical" mean? "Dialectical" is simply a fancy philosophy term that refers to the process of bringing together opposite ideas, so that you can see things from more or different perspectives.

DBT applies this idea of *dialectics* to emotional healing. Not surprising, DBT has many dialectics. The main dialectic of DBT is acceptance versus change. On one hand, healing requires you to accept yourself as you are. On the other hand, healing also requires you to change. Do you see how that is a dialectic? Even though these ideas seem like opposites, do you also see how both can be true at the same time? For example, deciding to accept yourself is already a change. In addition, you can't change something that you haven't accepted yet. In other words, even concepts that seem like opposites are sometimes two sides of the same coin!

Let's look at three more examples of dialectics that come out of the DBT philosophy: You are doing the best you can, but you also need to try harder; you are motivated to change, but you need to become even more motivated; maybe you didn't create all of your problems, but it's your responsibility to face them anyway. And that's just the beginning—there are many more.

In this book, you will be learning how to balance all kinds of dialectics. You will learn to balance overawareness versus underawareness, overthinking versus underthinking, overfeeling versus underfeeling, overreactions versus underreactions, and overdependence versus underdependence.

DBT has three simple goals: *Get out of hell, stay out of hell,* and *build a life worth living.* "Hell," in DBT lingo, refers to intense emotional pain. If you have invested in this workbook, then you probably have been in hell yourself, or maybe you know someone else who is. Many trauma survivors learn to successfully numb their pain—and then stop there. But that's not good enough for DBT! DBT is not *just* about reducing your emotional pain; it's not *just* about damage control; it's not *just* about cleaning up the rubble from Ground Zero. Rather, it's also about learning to laugh again, learning to love again, learning to live again—and learning to build a new tower.

DBT is unique as a treatment model in that this approach focuses almost exclusively on skills building. In this workbook, you will learn many specific skills related to the following themes: thoughts, feelings, behaviors, triggers, awareness, acceptance, and relationships. It takes a lot of time, work, patience, and self-forgiveness to learn new skills. You will not master a new skill overnight. On the contrary, you will probably make lots of SLIPS along the way. (Just remember, "SLIP" means Skills Learning In Progress.) *Any* attempt to do DBT *is* DBT. The *only* way to fail at DBT is to stop using it. (However, even if you decide to take a temporary break from DBT, you still did not fail. Rather, you just applied a DBT skill you'll learn in chapter 3 called the Mini Vacation!)

If you complete this entire workbook and find that you still have some symptoms of PTSD, that does not mean that DBT did not work or that you did not do this workbook correctly. On the contrary, what it might mean is that you need to consult with a professional counselor, preferably one that is trained in trauma work. A professional counselor might help you develop your DBT skills even further, or they might use a different model altogether. Either option is fine. DBT skills are highly compatible with other treatment approaches. In fact, DBT skills often lay the groundwork for ongoing or deeper trauma work. For example, DBT skills will help you manage your triggers, regulate your emotions, and stabilize your life, all of which are necessary conditions before attempting to process unresolved trauma.

THE EFFECTS OF TRAUMA

As previously mentioned, trauma has a way of throwing our lives out of sync in many different ways and directions. In this section, we will focus on how trauma affects two mental processes: *awareness* and *acceptance*.

When awareness and acceptance are altered enough, we enter into a mindless state. Two examples of mindlessness especially experienced by trauma survivors include *reactivity* and *dissociation*. These alterations to our mental processes are adaptive—and necessary—during periods of danger. But, unfortunately, these adaptions outlive the trauma itself—and, therefore, they also outlive their usefulness. That's why you will soon learn a skill called *mindfulness*, which helps us restore both awareness and acceptance to our daily lives.

Imbalanced Awareness

In the introduction, we discussed how trauma has a way of throwing us off balance by forcing our normal way of doing things to the extremes. One of the first things that trauma knocks off balance is our *awareness*.

When we experience trauma, we are forced to pay attention to things we wouldn't normally pay attention to. In particular, trauma causes us to focus on information that is directly related to our survival, while focusing less on everything else. For instance, if you are walking through the park and there is no reason to suspect any danger, you are likely to notice—and appreciate—the flowers, the birds, people walking their dogs, and children playing. But if you are walking through the park and you suddenly hear multiple gunshots, you will notice a completely different set of details—the sound of the gunfire, the direction of the shots, the closest place to duck for safety—and ignore everything that doesn't serve your safety.

Of course, our brain's ability to shift our awareness during periods of danger makes complete sense and is highly adaptive; without this ability, we would not be able to survive the trauma. However, our brain also seems to *overlearn* this tendency. Even after the trauma has long ended, our overall awareness remains altered, and we continue to *overfocus* on some details while *underfocusing* on others—even though our survival is no longer at stake. This ongoing altered awareness ends up causing lots of additional problems in our lives. We may even become obsessed with minor details while completely ignoring major problems.

Extreme Judgments

Not only does trauma force our awareness to the extremes, it also forces something else to the extremes: our *judgments*. When we experience trauma, everything becomes a matter of life and death, and we don't have a ton of time to distinguish between the two. Therefore, our brain makes quick, snappy judgments: good or bad, safe or unsafe, friend or foe.

Once again, the brain's ability to make rapid, simple judgments in times of danger is highly adaptive and allows us to survive the trauma. But the brain also seems to overlearn this tendency as well, which likewise causes even more ongoing problems down the road. With our extreme judgments overactivated, it is much more difficult to accept other perspectives, gray areas, or the middle ground. In other words, trauma does not just affect our awareness; it also affects our acceptance.

Mindlessness

To be *mindless* means to be unaware: of yourself, of others, of your thoughts and feelings, of your triggers and urges, of your reactions, and even of your judgments. And since you are unaware of your own judgments, you lack both awareness *and* acceptance whenever you are in a state of mindlessness.

Not surprisingly, there are many forms of mindlessness. However, people who have been traumatized tend to adopt two forms in particular: *reactivity* and *dissociation*.

"Reactivity" means to respond with our instincts or emotions without thinking first. Once again, this tendency is highly adaptive during periods of danger. We need to be reactive in order to survive a crisis. When we are in a life-or-death situation, we would be foolish to call all of our friends and ask for their opinions. However, this reactivity continues long after the trauma has stopped. In particular, trauma survivors tend to be very reactive to anything that reminds them (even remotely, indirectly, or subconsciously) of a previous trauma—which, not surprisingly, causes even more ongoing problems.

Dissociation literally means to disconnect from your own experiences. In other words, it means to "space out" for long periods of time. Dissociation is much more severe than simply daydreaming, which we all do at times. And you probably already know what I am going to say next: "Once again, this tendency is highly adaptive during periods of danger." In fact, the ability to mentally and emotionally disconnect from our own experiences during times of trauma is precisely what helps many people survive the trauma itself. But by now you already know this familiar tune: Asset then, liability now. Chronically disconnecting from our daily experiences is simply not an effective, long-term strategy for a happy, productive life.

But let's be clear: Since some states of mindlessness help us survive trauma, mindlessness truly is a *gift* of the mind (you won't hear too many DBT therapists tell you that!). However, mindlessness alone is also a rotten way to go through life. What if you were always reactive—to everything? What if you were always spacing out, even during your most cherished moments? What if you were always making quick, snappy, and sometimes very inaccurate judgments? That's why we also need the opposite of mindlessness, which is *mindfulness*.

WHAT IS MINDFULNESS?

Wouldn't it be amazing if there was something that could restore both awareness and acceptance back to their normal balance? Wouldn't it be amazing if you could notice—and even appreciate—flowers and birds and dogs and children in the park again, instead of focusing on every person you come across as the next armed attacker? Well, I have great news for you: There actually is a skill that teaches both awareness and acceptance at the same time! It's called *mindfulness*.

"Mindfulness" seems to be the latest buzzword in treatment circles, not to mention in society in general. But actually, the concept of mindfulness has been around for thousands of years.

When people hear the term "mindfulness," sometimes they think of meditation practices or great mystical experiences. While these activities might be examples of mindfulness, mindfulness is actually quite simple and ordinary. It is a concept that is readily accessible to everyone. While mindfulness does require patience and practice (just like anything good in life), it does not require decades of discipleship under a famous guru.

There are many definitions of mindfulness, but here is my favorite: *"To be aware, on purpose, in the present, without judging"* (adapted from Siegel 2007, 10). This definition has four distinct parts. Let's take a look at each of them in a little more detail:

1. To be aware

2. On purpose

3. In the present

4. Without judging

To Be Aware

"To be aware" simply means to notice, observe, or pay attention to something. We've already covered awareness and how trauma can throw it off balance. Now it's your turn to do some work! Grab a pen and answer these questions. Take your time and be honest with yourself.

How has trauma affected my awareness?

_____

_____

_____

_____

_____

_____

_____

_____

_____

_____

_____

_____

_____

_____

What are some things I notice now that I didn't notice before the trauma?

_____

_____

_____

_____

_____

_____

_____

_____

_____

_____

_____

_____

_____

_____

On Purpose

"On purpose" means to do something intentionally or deliberately, as opposed to randomly or accidentally. We all notice things when it's too late, or when we have no other choice but to notice them. However, many times we also fail to notice something when we do have a choice. And that's precisely why minor issues continue to build up over time; we never bother to notice them until minor issues have become major issues. That's one reason it is so important to learn to become more aware—*on purpose*.

What are some areas of my life that I no longer pay as much attention to as I should? (This list can include just about anything: spouse, children, work, finances, and so forth.)

_____

_____

_____

_____

_____

_____

_____

_____

_____

_____

How has ignoring these aspects of my life caused minor issues to become bigger issues?

_____

_____

_____

_____

_____

_____

_____

_____

_____

_____

In the Present

"In the present" means learning to focus on what's going on in the here and now. That does not mean that the past and future are not important. They are! However, here is one of the great ironies of life: *We cannot effectively heal from the past by obsessing about the past, nor can we effectively plan for the future by constantly worrying about the future.*

In fact, overthinking the *past* tends to drive *depression*, while overthinking the *future* tends to drive *anxiety*. And to make matters worse, when we do not intentionally try to focus on the present, our mind automatically gravitates to either the past or the future—or sometimes both at the same time.

However, by learning to become more grounded in the present, we are actually in a much better place to both heal from the past as well as plan for the future. But when we are not paying attention to what's going on in the here and now, we simply fumble from one crisis to the next, constantly reacting to skeletons from the past or phantoms of the future—without having a firm grasp on the reality that is right before our eyes. Perhaps you have heard the old adage: "Yesterday is history and tomorrow is a mystery, but today is a gift: And that's why we call it the present!"

Do I tend to obsess about the past or worry about the future? Provide some examples.

_____

_____

_____

_____

_____

_____

_____

_____

_____

_____

_____

_____

_____

_____

How has obsessing about the past caused feelings of depression in my life?

_____

_____

_____

_____

_____

_____

_____

_____

_____

How has too much worrying about my future caused feelings of anxiety in my life?

_____

_____

_____

_____

_____

_____

_____

_____

_____

_____

Does either obsessing about the past or worrying about the future help me deal with the present?

_____

_____

_____

_____

_____

_____

_____

_____

_____

_____

_____

How does becoming more aware of the present put me in a better place to deal with the present?

_____

_____

_____

_____

_____

_____

_____

_____

_____

_____

_____

How does becoming more aware of the present put me in a better position to heal from the past?

_____

_____

_____

_____

_____

_____

_____

_____

_____

_____

How does becoming more aware of the present put me in a better position to prepare for the future?

_____

_____

_____

_____

_____

_____

_____

_____

_____

_____

_____

To summarize so far, the first three components of mindfulness are all about awareness, specifically the *intentional awareness of the moment*—learning to deliberately notice, observe, and pay attention to events in the here and now. That's where mindfulness starts.

Without Judging

Now let's talk about the fourth component of mindfulness: "without judging." Now mindfulness just got a lot harder! How so? Well, imagine what will happen to us when we increase our intentional awareness of the present… We start to notice a whole lot of things that we wish we didn't see. In a sense, learning to become more mindful (more intentionally aware of the present) means letting go of our denial and other defense mechanisms. It means exposing ourselves to all the dirty laundry that we shoved under the bed. It means turning on the lights and seeing that the room is a mess. And what happens when we increase our awareness of things we would rather not see? We trigger our *judgments*!

Earlier in this chapter, we explained judgments as putting people and things into extreme categories: good or bad, safe or unsafe, friend or foe. Judgments are also the negative messages that go through our mind. Most of these negative messages probably came straight from people who were or are important to us. Over time, when we hear the same negative messages over and over again, they become internalized. In other words, they become our own negative messages, rattling through our heads.

The opposite of judgment is *acceptance*. A judgment basically screams: "Life should not be this way!" However, acceptance simply acknowledges: "But regardless, this is simply how things are right now." Now here's another great irony of life: Contrary to what seems logical, judgments do not actually make anything better. Think about it. When did judging yourself or someone else improve a situation? However, accepting a problem for what it is will actually put you in a better place to deal with the problem.

Therefore, mindfulness is not just about awareness. It is also about *acceptance*! The tricky part is increasing both awareness and acceptance at the same time.

How has trauma affected my acceptance? Have I started to put things in my life into distinct categories (such as good or bad, safe or unsafe, friend or foe)?

_____

_____

_____

_____

_____

_____

_____

_____

_____

_____

What are some of my judgments (or negative beliefs) about myself and others?

_____

_____

_____

_____

_____

_____

_____

_____

_____

Do these judgments make things better or worse for me?

_____

_____

_____

_____

_____

_____

_____

_____

_____

_____

_____

The Marriage of Awareness and Acceptance

So why is mindfulness so important? Why are awareness and acceptance such a big deal? The answer is simple. Under the best of conditions, life is full of problems. And what happens when we either ignore the problems or fail to accept them? Do they just go away? Do they get better all on their own? No, of course not! Awareness and acceptance are not just random, pointless exercises. Rather, they are the tools we need to deal with life. Once we become aware of our problems *and* accept our problems, we are in a much better place to deal with them. Only then are we finally in a position to decide if, when, and how to take action. But without awareness and acceptance, we continue to fumble through life just making problems worse.

Earlier in this chapter we learned that survivors of trauma experience alternations in both awareness and acceptance (resulting in mindless states, such as reactivity and dissociation). We also learned that dialectical behavior therapy is all about the process of finding balance by bringing together opposites. Therefore, one of the first opposites we need to balance is mindlessness versus mindfulness, since mindfulness is all about increasing both awareness and acceptance.

Remember how I mentioned that mindlessness is a gift to the brain because it helps us survive the trauma? Well, mindfulness is also a gift to the brain, since it helps us learn how to love and appreciate life again. The only hitch is that mindfulness is a gift that we have to learn and practice! Unlike mindlessness, mindfulness does not come to us naturally.

So what does *applied mindfulness* look like? So glad you asked! I've boiled it down to a very simple formula, which we will refer to throughout this workbook:

applied mindfulness = awareness + acceptance + action

Now, the beauty of this formula is that *awareness* plus *acceptance* are already *action*. In fact, just implementing awareness and acceptance is already more action than most people take in their daily lives! Therefore, sometimes awareness and acceptance are the only actions you need to apply to a situation— sometimes situations really do get better just by becoming more aware and more accepting of them. However, sometimes increased awareness plus increased acceptance also allow us to understand that further action is required. Either way, you are now in a more advantageous position to make better decisions moving forward.

PRACTICING MINDFULNESS

Make a habit of taking at least five minutes a day to intentionally pay attention to a specific activity. In other words, practice the skill of simply paying attention on purpose in the moment. As you pay attention to that activity, you might notice other thoughts, feelings, memories, sensations, urges, or interruptions pop into your awareness. Whenever you get distracted by something in your body, something in your mind, or something in your environment, simply acknowledge the distraction, and then return to whatever activity you were paying attention to.

Keep in mind that getting distracted does not mean you have failed at mindfulness: On the contrary, noticing your distractions is precisely what mindfulness is all about! In fact, one of the distractions you may experience might even be your own judgments for not being mindful enough. Well, guess what? As long as you notice your judgments, that is still mindfulness! The more you notice—and accept—both external and internal distractions (including and especially your own judgments), the less distracting the distractions become and the more your mindfulness increases.

You can practice mindfulness with just about anything! Here are some examples of ordinary, everyday activities with which you can start practicing mindfulness:

- Breathing
- Walking
- Eating
- Singing
- Praying
- Listening to music

- Listening to your spouse
- Washing dishes
- Exercising
- Watching a sunrise or sunset
- Playing an instrument
- Playing with your kids

Let's take a few of these activities to show how you can improve your mindfulness skills in just five minutes a day. As you will see with these examples, the same basic principles of mindfulness apply to any situation, no matter what activity you are using to practice.

Mindful Breathing

1. Find a quiet place. Remove any obvious distractions. Disconnect from technology.

2. Sit or lie in a comfortable position.

3. Start to notice your breathing cycle. Notice each breath as it comes in. Notice each breath as it goes out.

4. If your mind wanders, gently notice the wandering and then return to your breathing.

5. If you experience any other distraction, gently notice the distraction and then return to your breathing.

6. Try not to get so relaxed that you fall asleep. But if you do, then you did not fail at mindfulness... you just succeeded at relaxation!

Mindful Listening

1. Find a quiet place. Remove any obvious distractions. Disconnect from technology.

2. Both you and your partner should sit in a comfortable position.

3. Listen to each word that your partner says.

4. Look into your partner's eyes as they speak.

5. Notice each facial expression associated with each word.

6. As thoughts, feelings, and reactions are generated in your own mind, notice these experiences, and then gently refocus on each word that your partner speaks.

7. You will also notice possible responses to what your partner is saying. It's okay to notice these potential responses, but do not actually express them. Just notice them, and then gently refocus on each word your partner verbalizes.

Mindful Dishwashing

1. Kitchens are rarely quiet (at least not in my house), but try to remove any obvious distractions. Disconnect from technology.

2. Notice the flow and temperature of the water.

3. Notice the fragrance and feel of the detergent.

4. Notice the color, shape, texture, and size of each item in the sink.

5. Notice each physical sensation associated with washing dishes.

6. If your mind wanders, gently notice the wandering and then return to the dishes.

7. If you experience any other distraction, gently notice the distraction and then return to the dishes.

RAIN Dance

One of my favorite ways to apply mindfulness to my everyday life is what I call the RAIN Dance. RAIN stands for Recognize, Allow, Investigate, and Nurture. The RAIN Dance helps you apply the concepts of awareness and acceptance, as opposed to judgment. I especially like to use RAIN Dance when I am upset about something. First, I *recognize* signs of anger. For example, I might notice my fists start to clench. Next, instead of fighting the anger, I simply *allow* it to come and go as a wave. Then, instead of judging the anger, I *investigate* it by asking myself questions such as these: *I wonder why I am angry? I wonder what triggered me? I wonder why I am more upset than usual?* Finally, I *nurture* myself by using one of the coping strategies we will talk about in chapter 3, such as Controlled Breathing, Muscle Relaxation, or Mini Vacation.

Now try your own RAIN Dance. Think of an intense emotion, urge, or craving that you sometimes experience. Then respond to the following prompts.

1. **Recognize:** How do I know this feeling is coming? Where do I feel it in my body?

    _____

    _____

    _____

    _____

    _____

2. **Allow:** Imagine this feeling coming and going as a wave. How can I ride this wave instead of fighting it?

    _____

    _____

    _____

    _____

    _____

3. **Investigate:** Where did this feeling come from? Why I am feeling this now?

    _____

    _____

    _____

    _____

    _____

4. **Nurture:** What can I do to soothe myself? How can I take care of myself in this moment?

    _____

    _____

    _____

    _____

    _____

Practicing Applied Mindfulness

Think of an ongoing problematic situation in which you have not reacted effectively. This could be anything: conflict with a spouse, paying your bills, communicating with your children, and so forth. In this exercise, you will learn to handle this situation better by increasing your mindfulness of this situation. In particular, you will learn to apply mindfulness using the formula we learned earlier:

applied mindfulness = awareness + acceptance + action

Awareness

What have I failed to notice about this situation?

_____

_____

_____

_____

_____

_____

How has ignoring these details made the situation worse?

_____

_____

_____

_____

_____

What have I learned about this situation now that I am deliberately paying more attention?

_____

_____

_____

_____

_____

Acceptance

What are my judgments about this situation?

_____

_____

_____

_____

_____

How have these negative beliefs made the situation worse?

_____

_____

_____

_____

_____

_____

How will accepting this situation put me in a better position to deal with it?

_____

_____

_____

_____

_____

_____

Action

Based on my current awareness and current acceptance, is further action required?

_____

_____

_____

_____

_____

_____

If further action is required, what is my plan moving forward?

_____

_____

_____

_____

_____

How is my new response different than my original reaction?

_____

_____

_____

_____

_____

_____

To recap, we have learned that trauma affects two mental processes: *awareness* and *acceptance*. When awareness and acceptance are altered enough, we enter into a mindless state. Two examples of mindlessness especially experienced by trauma survivors include reactivity and dissociation. While both reactivity and dissociation are adaptive and necessary during periods of danger, they are not effective long-term strategies for the rest of life. Fortunately, we learned a skill called *mindfulness,* which helps us restore both awareness and acceptance to our daily lives.

Congratulations, you have just finished your first lesson! You are now taking your first bold steps toward applying mindfulness to your daily life!

THREE MINDS

Now that you have an introduction to mindfulness, let's delve into our next lesson and talk about the mind itself. Specifically, we are going to look at what the mind generates: *thoughts* and *feelings*. What are they, why do we need them, and what do we do with them? What if we only had thoughts and no feelings? What if we only had feelings but no thoughts? What if our thoughts made all the decisions? What if our feelings called all the shots? What if we didn't know what we were thinking or feeling in the first place? This lesson will answer all of these questions.

The Thinking Mind and the Feeling Mind

Let's start at the beginning: What are thoughts and what are feelings? To help answer this question, think of your favorite song. What are the lyrics of that song? Just like lyrics are the words running through a song, *thoughts* are like words running through your head. Now think of the music of your song. Can you describe all of the musical elements, such as the beat, rhythm, volume, harmony, melody, instrumentals, and so forth? Just as music sets the tone or mood for your song, *feelings*, or emotions, do the same thing: They set the tone or mood for your mind.

The same way your song has both words and music, your mind also has both thoughts and feelings. That means part of your brain does the thinking and part of your brain does the feeling. For the sake of simplicity, let's refer to these two parts of the mind as simply the *Thinking Mind* and the *Feeling Mind*.

The gift of the Thinking Mind is that it is *verbal*. Language is one of the most complicated things we do as humans. To this day, linguists cannot explain why or how little children can learn something so complex, so automatically, so fast, and so young—even while other parts of their brain have not developed yet! If you have ever tried to learn another language as an adult, then you know how complicated this process is. We use language every single day in just about everything we do. Even though a few other animals have limited forms of linguistic expression, the boundless capacity for verbal communication is one of the things that makes us distinctly human. In fact, human culture would never have advanced as much as it has without *words*.

But the gift of the Feeling Mind is that it is *nonverbal*. The Feeling Mind communicates just as much as the Thinking Mind—but without words. Scientists speculate that babies have emotions even before they are born (Parncutt 2015). That should not be surprising, since they certainly have emotions the second they come into this world! Since babies cannot talk yet, they use emotions to communicate, to motivate, and to influence others. And that ability never goes away: Throughout our lives, we continue to use emotions to communicate, motivate, and influence ourselves as well as others (Linehan 2015). In fact, even with our amazing gift of language, scientists point out that when verbal and nonverbal messages contradict each other, we still pay more attention to the nonverbal message (Frank 2016).

So which mind is more important? That's a trick question, since we need both! Let's assume you witness a tragic accident between two vehicles, and one of the drivers is badly injured. Let's first assume that you have a Feeling Mind but not a Thinking Mind. Would that be a good situation? Probably not, since you would be so consumed with so many overwhelming emotions that you might not know what to do. But now let's assume that you have a Thinking Mind but not a Feeling Mind. Would that be a good situation? The answer is still no. Even if you knew exactly what to do, would you even care about the injured person if you had no emotions at all? No, you would not, since you need emotions such as compassion and empathy to even care about helping someone else in the first place.

By now it should be clear that we need both the Thinking Mind and the Feeling Mind. But how do we use both of them at the same time?

The Balanced Mind

We can balance our Thinking Mind and Feeling Mind by bringing a third mind into play: the *Balanced Mind*. Throughout history, people have come up with many terms to describe the Balanced Mind. Some have called it intuition. Some have called it our conscience. Some have called it the soul. Regardless of your terminology, the Balanced Mind is the mind behind the mind; in other words, it's the part of the mind that supervises or oversees the rest of the mind.

The Balanced Mind has many useful functions. Here are some of them:

- **The Balanced Mind *identifies* our thoughts and feelings.** In other words, the Balanced Mind is the part of our brain that tells us what we are thinking and feeling in the first place.

- **The Balanced Mind *evaluates* what we are thinking and feeling.** In other words, the Balanced Mind is the unique part of the human mind that allows us to reflect on the other parts of the mind. The Balanced Mind allows us to think about thinking, to feel about feeling, and even to think about our feeling or feel about our thinking! Have you ever had a thought but then another thought told that thought that there was no evidence to back up the first thought? Or have you had a feeling but then another emotion let you know that you were uneasy with that feeling? Or have you felt guilty for having a particular thought? Or have you ever thought that a feeling was illogical? These are all examples of using the Balanced Mind to evaluate our thoughts and feelings.

- **The Balanced Mind helps us *regulate* our thoughts and feelings.** For instance, the Balanced Mind will tell us to stop obsessing about something if we have too many worry thoughts, or it will help tone down our emotions if they become too escalated.

- **The Balanced Mind helps us *balance* our thoughts and feelings.** Maybe you have noticed that sometimes your Thinking Mind and your Feeling Mind give you different messages. Perhaps your Thinking Mind is telling you, "You did nothing wrong," but your Feeling Mind feels guilty anyway. That's when your Balanced Mind will step in and balance your Thinking Mind and your Feeling Mind. For example, the Balanced Mind may decide: "You know, technically I did not do anything wrong, but I could have responded sooner, so it can't hurt to apologize for my role in this."

  Remember how we discussed that the process of dialectics is all about learning to balance opposites? Do you see how that's the job of the Balanced Mind? The Balanced Mind knows how to balance our thoughts and feelings, even if they are sending different messages. In addition, the Balanced Mind even knows how to find the balance between *overthinking* versus *underthinking* as well as *overfeeling* versus *underfeeling*. That's quite the balancing act! As we will see in later sections, the Balanced Mind also knows how to balance all kinds of other opposites as well.

- **The Balanced Mind learns how to make wise, balanced decisions by factoring in both our thoughts *and* our feelings.** After carefully analyzing both verbal and nonverbal input, a well-developed Balanced Mind always has several options. For example, the Balanced Mind may decide to side with the Thinking Mind. Or the Balanced Mind may decide to side with the Feeling Mind. Or the Balanced Mind may decide to compromise, integrate, or even transform the Thinking Mind and Feeling Mind (in other words, combine what the Thinking

Mind is saying and what the Feeling Mind is saying into a brand-new message). Regardless, the Balanced Mind will tend to make much better decisions than just the Thinking Mind or just the Feeling Mind alone. Of course, no one's Balanced Mind is perfect. However, the Balanced Mind gets better and better at making decisions over time, especially with practice and life experience.

WHEN THE BALANCED MIND LOSES ITS BALANCE

Tragically, some of us have learned to ignore the Balanced Mind. This can happen if we have received many *invalidating messages*, over and over, from other people. We are invalidated if someone else discounts some aspect of our experience. For example, if someone repeatedly tells us that we shouldn't feel a certain way or that our way of thinking is stupid, then we will stop paying attention to how we think or feel. In other words, we will stop using our Balanced Mind!

However, invalidating messages do not even have to contain words. In fact, some of the most invalidating messages are nonverbal. Abuse and neglect are examples of invalidating messages that directly imply that what we think or feel does not matter. Perhaps the most invalidating message of all is sexual abuse. Sexual abuse sends the message: "Nothing about you matters. Your thoughts do not matter. Your feelings do not matter. Your body does not matter. You do not matter mentally, emotionally, physically, spiritually, or sexually."

The research is clear that trauma is invalidating, and invalidation is traumatizing! On one hand, trauma causes you to distrust your own sense of reality. In fact, there's even a technical term for that: *derealization*. This happens when you no longer have a sense of what's real or unreal (American Psychiatric Association 2013). And when your own experiences do not even feel real to you, you have been invalidated. On the other hand, invalidation itself also causes trauma symptoms. For example, if you constantly hear messages that you don't matter, that you're worthless, that you should never have been born, you may develop some of the same exact symptoms as someone who has been raped. For example, you may have nightmares, flashbacks, and triggers associated with the invalidation (Linehan 2015).

Regardless, here's the bottom line when it comes to invalidation: Eventually, you come to believe the false or negative messages more than your own Balanced Mind. And as soon as you have learned to ignore your Balanced Mind, the results are tragic. Remember all of the roles and functions of the Balanced Mind? If you are not paying attention to your Balanced Mind, you no longer have any way to notice or regulate your thoughts and feelings. So that means you are basically at the mercy of whatever you happen to be thinking or feeling—but you do not even *know* what you are thinking or feeling in the first place! That's not a very good basis for making good decisions, is it?

Once we have stopped listening to our Balanced Mind…well, we lose our balance! In fact, there are four different directions in which can lose our balance:

- **We start to *overthink*.** This happens when we obsess about something over and over again.

- **We start to *underthink*.** This happens when we make reactive, impulsive decisions, without thinking first.

- **We start to *overfeel*.** This happens when we experience many overwhelming emotions all at once.

- **We start to *underfeel*.** This happens when we can't even feel our emotions at all; we just feel numb instead.

In fact, we can even experience all four tendencies at once: Some things we overthink while other things we underthink, and some things we overfeel while still other things we underfeel. I call this two different civil wars happening in our brain at the same time: The Thinking Mind is at war with itself by both overthinking and underfeeling, while the Feeling Mind is also at war with itself for underthinking and overfeeling. As you can see, the causalities of ignoring the Balanced Mind are pretty steep! That's why one major component of mindfulness is all about learning to pay attention to your Balanced Mind. Let's practice!

Learning to Mind the Minds: Thoughts, Feelings, and Balance

Think of a recent situation that happened in your personal life. This situation can be either positive or negative. Now let's analyze what each of your Three Minds told you about this situation.

Thinking Mind

What did my Thinking Mind communicate to me verbally? What were the words running through my head?

_____

_____

_____

_____

_____

_____

Did I overthink any aspect of this situation? For example, was my mind racing? Or did I have the same thoughts over and over? Or was it difficult to get my Thinking Mind to stop thinking?

_____

_____

_____

_____

_____

_____

Did I underthink any aspect of this situation? Did I miss important details or make impulsive decisions without having all the facts or all the evidence?

_____

_____

_____

_____

_____

Did any of my verbal messages seem to contradict each other?

_____

_____

_____

_____

_____

Did I engage in any sort of negative self-talk? What did I tell myself?

_____

_____

_____

_____

_____

How did any of these verbal messages from the Thinking Mind affect my Feeling Mind?

_____

_____

_____

_____

_____

Feeling Mind

How did my Feeling Mind communicate to me with emotions? Which emotions did I experience?

_____

_____

_____

_____

_____

_____

_____

Did I overfeel any aspect of this situation? Did my emotions seem more intense or overwhelming than the situation called for?

_____

_____

_____

_____

_____

_____

_____

Did I underfeel any aspect of the situation? Did I either deliberately or inadvertently numb any of my emotions? How so?

_____

_____

_____

_____

_____

_____

Did any of my emotions seem to contradict each other?

_____

What were my emotional triggers in this situation? In general, what are my emotional triggers?

_____

How did any of these emotional messages from my Feeling Mind affect my Thinking Mind?

_____

Congratulations! Whether you realize it or not, you have just used your Balanced Mind to analyze both your Thinking Mind and your Feeling Mind. Let's exercise your Balanced Mind even more by answering some additional questions. Let's keep rolling by keeping the same situation in mind.

Balanced Mind

Overall, does my Balanced Mind feel that I was overthinking or underthinking the situation? Is my Balanced Mind able to identify a more balanced way of thinking about the situation?

_____

_____

_____

_____

_____

Overall, does my Balanced Mind think that I was overfeeling or underfeeling the situation? Is my Balanced Mind able to identify a more balanced way of feeling about the situation?

_____

_____

_____

_____

_____

Did my Thinking Mind and my Feeling Mind send me different messages? Is my Balanced Mind able to balance these differences?

_____

_____

_____

_____

_____

_____

In this particular situation, does my Balanced Mind agree more with my Thinking Mind or more with my Feeling Mind?

_____

_____

_____

_____

_____

What has my Balanced Mind learned about this situation?

_____

_____

_____

_____

_____

Based on input from both my Thinking Mind and my Feeling Mind, how does my Balanced Mind plan to handle this situation in the future?

_____

_____

_____

_____

_____

In summary, in this lesson we have learned that we need both thoughts and feelings. Thoughts (which come from the Thinking Mind) contain verbal messages, while emotions (which come from the Feeling Mind) contain nonverbal messages. The role of the Balanced Mind is to notice, evaluate, regulate, and balance our thoughts and feelings—and then make balanced decisions.

However, we learn to stop listening to our Balanced Mind when we have experienced chronic invalidation, which is both a cause and an effect of trauma symptoms. And once we start ignoring the Balanced

Mind, we lose our balance by both overthinking and underthinking, as well as both overfeeling and underfeeling. In this lesson, you learned to pay more attention to your Balanced Mind so that you can restore balance to your life!

USING YOUR BALANCED MIND TO MEET YOUR NEEDS

So far in this chapter, we have defined mindfulness as the marriage between awareness and acceptance. We have seen that it is especially important to learn how to be intentionally aware of—and accepting of—the present moment. We have also seen that it is difficult to increase both awareness and acceptance at the same time, since sometimes the more aware we become, the more we see the things we wish we didn't see. However, we have also seen that it pays to increase both awareness and acceptance, because that puts us in a better place to deal with life. In other words, awareness and acceptance help us know how to take action, if necessary.

In this lesson, we will continue to develop the Balanced Mind to increase our mindfulness of the basic needs we have as people. In short, we are going to learn to become more aware of our needs *and* more accepting of our needs, which in turn will help us learn how to actually meet those needs more effectively.

As we begin this lesson, keep the mindfulness formula in mind:

applied mindfulness = awareness + acceptance + action

Maslow Builds a Pyramid

In 1940, a famous psychologist named Abraham Maslow identified five basic levels of needs we have as people. He placed these need levels into a pyramid. The lower levels in the pyramid represent the needs that are most necessary for survival, while the higher ones represent the needs that are most necessary for us to fully develop as humans.

Maslow observed a few interesting patterns with these need levels. First, he noticed that the brain tends to focus more on unmet needs than needs that have been satisfied. Second, Maslow noticed that if multiple needs are unmet, the brain tends to focus more on the lower needs—the needs more necessary for survival. In other words, if too many needs remain unmet, the brain starts to go into survival mode, rather than focusing on the process of thriving (Maslow 2013).

Let's look at these five levels of needs, starting from the bottom and working our way up. The first level of the pyramid represents our *physical and medical needs*. This is what we absolutely need to stay alive: the basics such as food, clothing, and shelter. Once our basic biological needs have been met, our mind then turns to the next level of the pyramid, which represents needs related to *safety and security*. I personally make a distinction between *physical* safety versus *emotional* security. Sometimes we are physically *safe* but not emotionally *secure*. Therefore, if emotional abuse is present, these needs are not being met.

Once we feel safe and secure, our mind next turns to needs related to *love and belonging*. I personally make another distinction between feeling connected to one person (love) versus feeling included by a group (belonging). As people, we need both: We have a deep need for strong one-on-one attachments, and we also have a strong need to feel a part of something bigger than ourselves.

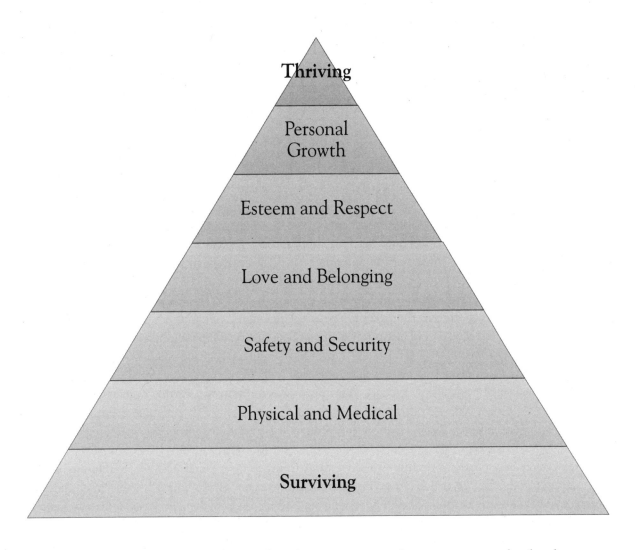

Once our needs for love and belonging have been met, our mind next turns to needs related to *esteem and respect*. I personally make another distinction between these terms: *Esteem* refers to how we see ourselves, while *respect* refers to how other people treat us. As children, we learn to see ourselves based on how we are treated by others. If our caregivers treat us well (respect), we learn to have a healthy and balanced view of ourselves (esteem). However, if our caregivers do not respect us, we are likely to experience lower self-esteem.

Finally, once our needs for esteem and respect are met, our mind then turns to the highest level of needs, which Maslow called *self-actualization*. This is simply a fancy term that refers to feeling fulfilled, meeting our full potential, achieving our goals, or performing at the top of our game. That's why I refer to self-actualization as our need for *personal growth*.

How Trauma Affects the Pyramid

So where are we going with all of this? Trauma survivors, by definition, have experienced unmet needs. Perhaps some of your biological needs were neglected. Or maybe you were physically threatened or emotionally abused. Or maybe you were rejected by your family or peers. Or maybe you were told that you were worthless.

What happens to us when our needs are not met? Recall the two principles discovered by Maslow: (1) Our mind tends to focus on unmet needs more than met needs. (2) When multiple needs are not met, the brain tends to focus more on the lower needs. In other words, when one or more of the first four need levels are not met, that's what our brain focuses on. And that's when we go into survival mode by investing our time and energy into meeting our needs—as opposed to developing our talents, gifts, and interests. In short, we adopt a *reactive, needs-based orientation* as opposed to a *proactive, strengths-based orientation*. We are no longer focused on reaching our full potential, meeting our goals, or performing at the top of our game.

Let's use a simple example to illustrate how this process works. Let's assume you have a huge project due at work. Now let's also assume that you have been sick but cannot afford to visit the doctor (biological need). To make matters worse, your partner just came home drunk, increasing his potential for domestic violence (safety and security). Not only that, but your mother-in-law just told you, "We never wanted you in this family in the first place" (love and belonging). And to top it off, your intoxicated partner just called you a "worthless slut" (esteem and respect). How much of your brain will be free to focus on your work project? Do you see how your mind will naturally gravitate toward all of these unmet needs? Even if you successfully dissociate from all of these problems, you might also dissociate from the work project.

And to make matters worse, most of us are not very good at meeting our needs all by ourselves. In fact, we often create more problems than we started with by trying to meet our needs in ways that are ineffective, counterproductive, or maladaptive. Just think of how many of our impulsive, reactive, and self-destructive habits (such as drugs, drinking, binging, and unsafe sex) are actually maladaptive attempts to meet our needs.

So how do we turn all of this around? Let's apply the all-important formula:

applied mindfulness = awareness + acceptance + action

Meeting My Needs Mindfully

This exercise will help you become more aware of your needs *and* more accepting of your needs, both of which will help put you in a better position to actually meet your needs more effectively.

Awareness

First, let's become more aware of your needs.

Were my basic survival meets ever unmet? Which ones?

_____

_____

_____

_____

_____

_____

Was there ever a time when I did not feel physically safe? Describe:

_____

_____

_____

_____

_____

_____

Was there ever a time when I did not feel emotionally secure? Describe:

_____

_____

_____

_____

_____

_____

Was there ever a time when I did not feel loved? Describe:

_____

_____

_____

_____

_____

_____

Was there ever a time when I did not feel like I belonged? Describe:

_____

_____

_____

_____

_____

_____

Esteem is how we see ourselves. What is one example of a negative message that I tell myself?

_____

_____

_____

_____

_____

Respect is how other people see me. What is one example of how someone else disrespected me?

_____

_____

_____

_____

_____

_____

What is one example of how the way someone treated me affected the way I see myself?

_____

_____

_____

_____

_____

_____

Acceptance

Now let's practice accepting your needs by exploring why each of these needs is so important.

Why is it necessary for our biological needs to be met to reach our full potential?

_____

_____

_____

_____

_____

_____

Why do we need to feel both safe and secure in order to reach our full potential?

_____

_____

_____

_____

_____

_____

Why do we need to feel loved by at least one person in order to reach our full potential?

_____

_____

_____

_____

_____

Why do we need to feel like we belong to a group to reach our full potential?

_____

_____

_____

_____

_____

Why do we need to feel esteem and respect to reach our full potential?

_____

_____

_____

_____

_____

Was I ever forced to sacrifice my plans, goals, and dreams to meet another need? Describe:

_____

_____

_____

_____

_____

_____

Action

Now that you have increased both awareness and acceptance of your needs, let's take some action!

Which of my needs are not currently being met?

_____

_____

_____

_____

_____

Have I ever attempted to meet any of my needs in unhealthy ways?

_____

_____

_____

_____

_____

Identify five of my problem behaviors. Which needs am I trying to meet with each of these behaviors?

Problem behavior: _____

_____

_____

_____

_____

Need(s): _____

_____

_____

_____

_____

_____

Problem behavior: _____

_____

_____

_____

_____

_____

Need(s): _____

_____

_____

_____

_____

_____

Problem behavior: _____

_____

_____

_____

_____

_____

Need(s): _____

_____

_____

_____

_____

_____

Problem behavior: _____

_____

_____

_____

_____

_____

Need(s): _____

_____

_____

_____

_____

_____

Problem behavior: _____

_____

_____

_____

_____

_____

Need(s): _____

_____

_____

_____

_____

_____

What are healthier ways of meeting these same needs?

Need: _____

New behavior: _____

_____

Need: _____

New behavior: _____

_____

Need: _____

New behavior: _____

_____

Need: _____

New behavior: _____

_____

Need: _____

_____

New behavior: _____

_____

According to Maslow, the highest need we have is to feel fulfilled or to become the very best we can be at something. Describe my goals, plans, and dreams for the future.

_____

_____

_____

_____

_____

_____

_____

_____

To recap, in this lesson we have learned to become more aware—and accepting—of our needs. First, we learned that we have five basic levels of needs, ranging from surviving (just staying alive) to thriving (reaching our full potential). In addition, we learned that our brain tends to focus more on unmet needs than met needs; and when multiple needs are not met, our brain tends to focus more on the needs most required to survive. In other words, when too many of our needs are unmet, we start to focus more on surviving and less on thriving. However, thriving is still a need we have; in fact, according to Maslow, it is the highest need we have! That's why, in the next and final section of this chapter, we are going to devote an entire lesson to just that: setting goals to reach your full potential.

USING THE BALANCED MIND TO MAKE YOUR GOALS

According to Maslow's pyramid of basic needs, the highest need we have as people is to set—and meet—our goals. That's why we are going to conclude this chapter with an entire lesson on this one single need: your goals for life and treatment!

There are many studies on how setting goals improves performance, both in school and at work. But setting goals can also help with trauma. One study found that setting goals significantly helped reduce trauma symptoms, even in combat-related chronic PTSD (Avraham et al. 1992). And research shows that goals are even better when they are SMART: Specific, Measurable, Attainable, Relevant, and Time-based (adapted from Scott 2017).

Let's assume one goal you have for yourself is to become a better student. While this is a great goal, there are some problems with it. First, this goal does not tell you how you will know when you are a better student. Second, this goal also does not tell you what you need to do in order to become a better student. So let's turn "become a better student" into a SMART goal, and see what happens.

How about this instead: "I will bring up all of my grades to a C or higher by turning in all of my homework, reviewing my notes after class, studying for a half hour every day, studying for one hour if there is a test, and asking for extra help if I need it." Do you see how this new goal has elements that make the general goal more specific, measurable, attainable, relevant, and time-oriented? Research shows that we are much more likely to meet our goals when they are SMART.

Setting SMART Goals

Take a look at the following areas of your life, and rate each of these domains on a scale of 1 to 10. A 10 means that everything is perfect in that area of your life; a 1 means that aspect of your life is absolutely miserable and could not get any worse. Place your numeric score in the narrow middle column. Next, identify the areas of your life that you most want to work on. This might be a really low-ranking domain, or it just might be an aspect of your life that's going fairly well but that you feel needs some progress. Put a star next to each goal that you want to focus on as you work your way through this workbook. Finally, in the last column, write down a brief note describing what it would take to make that particular area of your life a perfect 10.

Important Life Domains	Score (1–10)	SMART Goals (Specific, Measurable, Attainable, Relevant, Timely)
Stress and Coping		
Work and Finances		
Friends and Peers		
Dating and Romance		
Parents and Caregivers		
Feelings and Emotions		
Hobbies and Interests		
Marriage and Relationships		

School and Study		
Probation and Parole		
Body Image		
Thoughts About Self		
Other Thoughts		
Drugs and Alcohol		
Other Habits		
Other Important Areas		

Congratulations! You now have created SMART goals to guide you through the rest of this workbook. Keep these goals in mind as you complete the rest of the exercises in the remaining chapters.

THE LAST WORD

In this chapter, we learned that trauma throws us off balance by forcing us to the extremes. This process especially affects our awareness, our acceptance, our thoughts, and our feelings. For example, trauma causes us to pay more attention to some details while ignoring other details. In addition, trauma causes us to both overthink and underthink as well as both overfeel and underfeel. Trauma also activates our judgments, which makes us less accepting of the gray areas of life. Finally, trauma (by definition) means that our experiences have been invalidated and that some of our needs have not been met—including the need we all have to be productive, constructive, and to reach our full potential.

Clearly, trauma causes a lot of issues! Where do we even start to restore our sense of balance? A fantastic place to start is with a skill called mindfulness. We defined mindfulness as "paying attention, on purpose, in the present, without judging." We learned that this definition includes two components: awareness and acceptance. We also learned that the Balanced Mind is the part of the mind that knows how to be mindful, and therefore knows how to restore balance to our lives. As we become more aware *and* more accepting of our thoughts, feelings, and needs, we are in a better position to take action. Not only that, but something else we learned in this chapter is that the highest need we have as humans is to reach our full potential. And that's precisely why we ended this chapter with a lesson on setting goals to guide you through the rest of this workbook—and life!

CHAPTER 2

Restoring Balance with Awareness, Acceptance, Action

In the first chapter, we learned that mindfulness is all about learning to "pay attention, on purpose, in the present moment, without judging." Essentially, mindfulness includes both awareness *and* acceptance. We also learned that it pays to become more aware and more accepting, because both habits put us in a better position to deal with life—in other words, to take action. That's why we identified the mindfulness formula as:

applied mindfulness = awareness + acceptance + action

In this chapter, we will expand each of these themes. In particular, we will see that awareness, acceptance, and action are not as simple as switches that we just turn on and off. On the contrary, we might be more aware of some issues than other issues; we might be more accepting of some problems than other problems; and we might be more willing to take action with some behaviors than other behaviors.

Because life is so difficult, awareness, acceptance, and action can also be difficult. For instance, maybe you would prefer *not* to be aware of an issue; maybe you would prefer *not* to accept a problem; or maybe would you prefer *not* to take action. That's why awareness, acceptance, and action often happen gradually, in layers. In this chapter, you will learn about different fields of awareness, different stages of acceptance, and different levels of action.

FIELDS OF AWARENESS

Have you ever noticed something about someone else before that person did? Maybe that person has a funny tic or says the word "like" way too many times in one sentence. On the flip side, have you ever thought that other people might notice things about you that you don't even realize about yourself?

In this lesson, we are going to talk about four different fields of awareness (Davies 2014):

Field 1: Information that others know about me *and* that I know about myself.

Field 2: Information that others know about me *but* that I do not know about myself.

Field 3: Information that I know about myself *but* that others do not know about me.

Field 4: Information that others do not know about me *and* that I do not know about myself.

	Known to Self	**Unknown to Self**
Known to Others	Field 1 **OPEN**	Field 2 **BLIND**
Unknown to Others	Field 3 **HIDDEN**	Field 4 **MYSTERY**

Field 1 refers to *general* or *public information*, since this is information that both you and others know about yourself. For example, most people within your social circles probably know your name, your job, where you live, how many kids you have, and so forth. Field 1 is usually the stuff of small talk.

Field 2 refers to *blind spots*; this is information that other people know about you, but you do not know about yourself. As uncomfortable as this may seem, everyone has blind spots. We simply cannot observe ourselves from the same perspective as everyone else. Even when we look in a mirror, we still cannot see ourselves to the same extent as someone else looking at us. Therefore, people end up observing details about us that we do not even realize.

Blind spots become a major issue in our lives when we have problems that other people see but we do not. Trauma survivors can have unique blind spots. For example, some of your reactions may seem like overreactions to other people. Or some of your triggers may seem illogical to other people. Or some of your intense emotions may seem out of proportion to other people.

One goal of this workbook is to help you identify your blind spots.

Field 3 refers to *hidden information*, since this is information that you know about yourself, but others do not. Not here's the tricky part about hidden information: Some information is just personal and we should keep it private, because other people don't always need to know all of our business. However, some information is toxic when we keep it private, and we should share this information with someone we trust. In other words, there is a difference between *healthy* versus *unhealthy* secrets. Examples of unhealthy *secrets* include any past or present abuse, neglect, or trauma. We were not designed as people to carry these burdens alone!

Another goal of this workbook is for you to identify any traumatic experiences (either past or present) that you need to process.

Field 4 refers to the unknown; this is information that nobody knows about—yet! However, as you continue to journey through this workbook (as well as life), information from this field will start to transfer to the other fields. The more you practice the skills in this workbook, the more you will learn about yourself and the more others will learn about you as well!

What's in Your Field?

Answer the following questions about yourself.

What are three things that most people know about me?

_____

_____

_____

What are some of my blind spots from the past?

_____

_____

_____

_____

_____

Is it possible that I still might have some blind spots? If so, what might they be?

_____

_____

_____

_____

_____

What are some examples of unhealthy secrets from my past?

_____

_____

_____

_____

_____

Do I still have some unhealthy secrets that may need to come out? Do I feel comfortable sharing them with a trusted friend or counselor?

_____

_____

_____

_____

_____

Life is a mystery! What are some aspects of myself that I would like to learn more about?

_____

_____

_____

_____

_____

_____

What did I learn about myself from this exercise?

_____

_____

_____

_____

_____

_____

_____

Congratulations, you have just increased your self-awareness! Not only have you identified some of your blind spots, you have also identified hidden information that needs to be processed, perhaps with a professional therapist. In the next two lessons, we will learn how to overcome two special kinds of blind spots: *denial* and *pre-contemplation*.

STAGES OF ACCEPTANCE

All of us struggle at times to accept the reality we have been dealt. Sometimes reality is so painful we would rather pretend that some things do not exist or never happened. Trauma survivors have even harsher realities to accept than most people. Just accepting the trauma itself is hard enough! But that's not all. You also have to accept how the trauma has affected all aspects of your life: your thoughts, your emotions, your behaviors, and your relationships. Healing from trauma requires you to accept (*not* agree with, but *accept*) not only the trauma itself but all the ways that the trauma has affected your life now.

Sometimes reality is so harsh that we simply cannot accept all of it at once. That's when we gradually process reality in stages. Sometimes we pass through several phases of nonacceptance before we finally reach a place of acceptance. This is perfectly normal and healthy—as long as we are progressing toward full acceptance. Unfortunately, life only gets much more difficult when we get stuck for too long on any of the forms of nonacceptance. Nobody that I know is going to tell you that acceptance is easy. But one thing I can assure you: Nonacceptance is even harder!

There are five well-known stages many of us go through as we attempt to process reality: denial, anger, bargaining, depression, and acceptance (Kübler-Ross 2014).

Denial

Sometimes traumatic events are so horrendous and so unexpected that our first reaction is shock and disbelief. In other words, *denial*!

Let's use a surgery example to illustrate how denial (and the four other stages) can play out in our lives. What happens when we have surgery and the pain of the operation is too difficult to bear? The medical staff will administer some sort of numbing agent. The numbing agent doesn't remove the source of the pain; it just temporarily blocks the pain. Denial is like a drug that numbs out reality when it is too painful for us to deal with. Denial is our mind's way of protecting us when we can't handle a full dose of reality yet. While we sometimes need this "mental anesthesia" (at least initially), too much denial can obviously create additional issues of its own. Trauma survivors sometimes engage in activities or consume substances that further numb the pain.

Example: My boyfriend beats me because he loves me. This is how he shows me that I am his woman.

Connections: Remember the Thinking Mind, Feeling Mind, and Balanced Mind? When an individual is in the denial stage, all three minds are deactivated. While this complete shutdown may be temporarily appropriate, it is not a good long-term solution. Do you also remember our previous discussion on blind spots? Denial is a great example of not seeing information about ourselves that other people do.

Reality check: What sorts of problems can happen when you are in denial mode?

_____

_____

_____

Anger

What happens when the anesthesia wears off after a surgery? Now we feel the pain, don't we? The same exact principle applies once our denial or "mental anesthesia" wears off. We feel the emotional pain triggered by the situation. In other words, we feel *anger*.

But anger, like a drug, has an important function, within limits: It can provide us with the impulse and energy to change the traumatic situation. But what if the original situation can no longer be changed? Now what's going to happen to all that anger? Not surprising, too much anger can create additional issues of its own. Trauma survivors tend to have lots of anger simmering just beneath the surface—a simmer that quickly turns to a boil when triggered.

Example: The next time my boyfriend lays a hand on me, I am going to cut myself to show him how ticked I am! (This is an example of turning anger toward yourself, which can be common among trauma survivors.)

Connections: When an individual is in the anger stage, the Thinking Mind and Balanced Mind are both deactivated, but the Feeling Mind is in full throttle. While this arrangement may be temporarily appropriate, it is not a good long-term solution.

Reality check: What sorts of problems can happen when you are in anger mode?

_____

_____

_____

Bargaining

Once both of these "drugs" (denial and anger) wear off, we become slightly more rational. In fact, we might even start to think too much! *Bargaining* is when we try to scheme, negotiate, or manipulate our way out of a situation. While this may sometimes be a good strategy, what if no amount of scheming, negotiating, or manipulating will change the original trauma?

Let's continue our surgery analogy. Let's assume we try to convince ourselves and/or our doctors that our life would be so much better if only we were prescribed more pain medications, or the doctor placed us on disability, or we could sue someone, or… The problem with too much bargaining is that it is full of unrealistic, ineffective, and wishful thinking or plans. That's why too much bargaining can create additional issues as well.

Example: Maybe I just need to be a better girlfriend. Maybe I just need to learn to not tick him off so much. Maybe if I can make it up to him, this won't happen again. Maybe…

Connections: When an individual is in the bargaining stage, the Feeling Mind and Balanced Mind are both deactivated, but the Thinking Mind is in full throttle. While this arrangement may be temporarily necessary, it is not a good long-term solution.

Reality check: What sorts of problems can happen when you are in bargaining mode?

_____

_____

_____

Depression

Once our attempts to bargain have failed, we feel helpless and hopeless. The doctor has not prescribed more pain meds, there is no way to get on disability, and our boss wants us back on the job in three weeks. We feel that we are stuck, with no way out. We feel as if things will never ever get better. We even start to feel worthless, like we somehow deserve to be in this situation. In other words, we feel *depressed.*

Depression feels the worst but is also the closest to acceptance, because we finally start to see just how bad the circumstances really are. Remember, "It's always darkest before dawn." Of course, too much depression can create further issues as well. One problem with depression is that the situation that we're in, as awful as it might be, can now seem even worse. In other words, depression tends to make things seem more personal, permanent, and pervasive than they really are. *Personal* means that bad things happen to you because you are a bad person. *Permanent* means that the bad things will never go away. And *pervasive* means *everything* is now dark and bleak—not just the trauma. Another problem with depression is that we lose the ability and energy to deal with the rest of life.

Example: This is just how he is. He will always be abusive. I will never be good enough for him. But, of course, I was never good enough for him in the first place. I guess I should just be thankful that at least some guy wants me. This is all I deserve anyway…

Connections: When an individual is in the depression stage, the Feeling Mind and Thinking Mind are both activated, but the Balanced Mind is not! And since the Balanced Mind is not active, negative thoughts and negative emotions continue to feed off each other, resulting in a dark, gloomy cyclical cloud of depression. While this arrangement may be temporarily appropriate, it is not a good long-term solution.

Reality check: What sorts of problems can happen when you are in depression mode?

Acceptance

Acceptance happens when we fully acknowledge and embrace the circumstances just as they really are (no better and no worse). It has been said, "Acceptance…is the only way out of hell" (Linehan 2015, 420). When we finally face reality as it is, we can actually do something about it!

Example: My boyfriend is abusive. This is an abusive relationship. I have options. I deserve better than this!

Connections: When an individual is in the acceptance stage, all three minds are active: Thinking Mind, Feeling Mind, and Balanced Mind. Since we have access to the Feeling Mind, we still feel the pain of the trauma, but it is no longer so overwhelming. And since we have access to the Thinking Mind, we see the facts more clearly and rationally. But most important, since we have access to the Balanced Mind, we know how to accept the trauma, deal with the trauma, heal from the trauma, and move on with the rest of our life!

Reality check: Life is never perfect, even when we have mastered the art of acceptance. What sorts of problems can still happen even when you are in acceptance mode?

Of course, nobody progresses through the five stages perfectly. Sometimes we do not go through these stages in this exact order. Sometimes we experience more than one stage at the same time. For example, you might experience anger and bargaining at the same time; even denial and depression can overlap. Sometimes we regress in the stages. And sometimes one of these stages is our default response to any life trigger.

Learning acceptance does not mean you will never experience any of the roadblocks of denial, anger, bargaining, or depression. Rather, the key to acceptance is learning what your particular roadblocks are and how to overcome them. Remember, each of these forms of nonacceptance is normal and has its place—but none of these roadblocks is a healthy place to camp out long term. So the next time you experience denial, anger, bargaining, or depression, ask yourself: *Is this a roadblock keeping me stuck? Or is this a stepping-stone leading me toward acceptance?*

Identifying Stages of Acceptance

Think of a situation from the past that was really difficult for you to accept, but do not choose the worst trauma you have ever experienced. This can be a situation that you either ultimately accepted or still have not fully accepted.

Provide an example of when it was difficult to accept something.

_____
_____
_____
_____
_____
_____
_____
_____

Did I experience any denial? _____

• What did my denial look like? _____
_____
_____

• What additional problems were caused by the denial? _____
_____
_____
_____

Did I experience any anger? _____

• What did my anger look like? _____
_____
_____
_____

- What additional problems were caused by the anger? _____
_____
_____
_____

Did I experience any bargaining? _____

- What did my bargaining look like? _____
_____
_____
_____

- What additional problems were caused by the bargaining? _____
_____
_____
_____

Did I experience any depression? _____

- What did my depression look like? _____
_____
_____
_____

- What additional problems were caused by the depression? _____
_____
_____
_____

Was I able to finally accept the difficult situation? If no, why not? If so, how did I accept it?
_____
_____
_____

Now think of areas in your life that you are currently struggling to accept.

What is one area of my life in which I currently have too much denial? _____ _____

_____

_____

_____

- How is denial getting in the way of acceptance? _____

_____

_____

_____

- How is denial causing more problems for me? _____

_____

_____

_____

What is one area of my life in which I currently have too much anger? _____

_____

_____

_____

- How is anger getting in the way of acceptance? _____

_____

_____

_____

- How is anger causing more problems for me? _____

_____

_____

_____

What is one area of my life in which I currently have too much bargaining? _____

_____

_____

_____

- How is bargaining getting in the way of acceptance? _____

  _____

  _____

  _____

- How is bargaining causing more problems for me? _____

  _____

  _____

  _____

What is one area of my life in which I currently have too much depression? _____

_____

_____

_____

- How is depression getting in the way of acceptance? _____

  _____

  _____

  _____

- How is depression causing more problems for me? _____

  _____

  _____

  _____

Make a list of all the things in my life that I currently need to accept.

_____

_____

_____

_____

_____

_____

_____

What are my primary roadblocks to acceptance? Select however many apply.

- Denial

- Anger

- Bargaining

- Depression

What are some practical ways of overcoming these roadblocks?

- Denial:_____

  _____

  _____

  _____

- Anger: _____

  _____

  _____

  _____

- Bargaining: _____

  _____

  _____

  _____

- Depression: _____

_____

_____

_____

Congratulations! You have just learned to both identify and overcome the four major roadblocks of full acceptance: denial, anger, bargaining, and depression. Since no one immediately and fully accepts painful events all at once, it is perfectly normal to experience these various forms of nonacceptance. However, none of these forms of nonacceptance is a good long-term strategy for life. That's why in this lesson we learned how to continue our journey toward full acceptance.

LEVELS OF ACTION

Now that we know how to recognize—and overcome—the obstacles to acceptance, we can next focus on taking action.

In the previous lesson, we talked about the importance of accepting the original trauma as well as the effects of the trauma. As you may recall, trauma affects us in many ways: our emotions, our thoughts, our relationships, and our behaviors. Sometimes one of the most difficult things to accept is that our own behaviors, as a result of the trauma, have not always been the healthiest. Well, as it turns out, our own behaviors are not just difficult to accept—they can be even more difficult to change!

In this lesson, we are going to focus on the five stages of taking action: pre-contemplation, contemplation, preparation, change, and maintenance (Connors et al. 2015).

Pre-contemplation

To contemplate means to think about something. Therefore, *pre-contemplation* refers to a time before you are even thinking about how your behavior might be a problem. Notice that pre-contemplation resembles denial. Just like acceptance starts with overcoming denial, action also starts with overcoming pre-contemplation. Pre-contemplation is another example of a blind spot: Other people often notice what needs to change before we do.

Example: I'm not sure why the wife is always on my case. Joe drinks way more than I do, and his wife never complains about it!

Contemplation

Remember, contemplation is the act of thinking about something. Therefore, *contemplation* refers to a time when you start thinking about your behavior. Contemplation does not mean that you are necessarily convinced the behavior is a problem, just that you start to think more about the behavior and how it may or may not be problematic.

Have you ever heard the phrase "paralysis through analysis"? The problem with too much contemplation is that it resembles constipation: There's no movement!

Example: I've called in "sick" five times this month. Now my boss *and* my wife are on my case. I can't pack down my liquor like the good ol' days. Must be getting older!

Preparation

This stage is all about getting ready to potentially deal with the behavior. This stage implies that you have already thought long and hard about the behavior, and you have decided that something needs to give. You would finally like to change something. At the very least, you start to make some internal or mental changes. Or maybe you have even taken some baby steps to help change at least some aspects of the problem behavior.

Example: I have got to find a way to get everyone off my back. That's it: No more drinking till Friday night. I am not going to stop at the bar on my way home from work. And that hidden stash of booze in the closet has gotta go…

Change

This stage is all about finally doing something visibly different in your behavior that other people can actually observe. At first blush, it seems like you have arrived at your destination. After all, you have finally changed your problem behavior. Everyone should celebrate…right? Not yet.

The change stage is still full of landmines. Many people let down their guard when they reach this stage. They think that they have the problem licked. They start to take "harmless" risks as they allow themselves more and more freedom. That's why people with too much overconfidence tend to experience relapse at this stage.

Example: Okay, so only drinking on Fridays didn't work. I think I just need to bid farewell to my long and storied drinking career. Out with the Old Me. In with the New Upgrade: Clean and Sober! Now I will be attending AA meetings on Friday evenings! [*Fast-forward:*] Now that I have a month of sobriety under my belt, surely my sponsor won't mind if I head over to Joe's apartment for his birthday bash. Maybe I can even brag about how sober I've been…

Maintenance

As you can see, it's not enough to change just one time; change needs to be maintained! That's why the last stage of action is when you have not only made the decisive change but have also found ways to successfully maintain the new behavior over time. Regression back to old habits is still always possible, but now you realize that. Therefore, you have found ways to avoid relapse—and get back on track right away if you do slip up.

Example: After a few painful relapses back in my early days of sobriety, I have now been abstinent for five years. I have learned the key to maintaining my sobriety is to avoid certain people, places, and things—and never to miss an AA meeting!

Working through the levels of action is a lot like working through the stages of acceptance: Nobody goes through the levels perfectly; not everyone goes through these levels in this exact order; it is possible to go through different levels at the same time; and it is also possible to regress in the levels.

Here's one analogy that has always helped me to understand the stages of action—and especially the importance of making it all the way to maintenance. Let's assume that someday you would like to have a garden full of vegetables. However, right now it's February, and you are not even thinking about the garden yet. That's *pre-contemplation*. How many vegetables will you have if you stay in this stage?

Now let's assume it's March, and you finally start to think about the garden. You think about what kinds of tools, soil, and seeds you will need. That's *contemplation*. But how many vegetables will you have if you stay in this stage?

Now let's assume it's April, and you start to get everything ready for the garden: You buy the tools, the soil, and the seeds. You even rototill a little plot of ground. That's *preparation*. But how many vegetables will you have if you stay in this stage?

Now let's assume it's May. You finally plant the garden! That's the *change* stage. Congratulations!

But now let's assume you do absolutely nothing to *maintain* this garden for the rest of the summer. You don't water. You don't weed. You don't fertilize. How many vegetables should you expect by the end of August if you stay in this stage?

Now do you see the importance of making it all the way to maintenance? Lifelong changes are not onetime deals: They need to be maintained!

Taking Action

Think of a behavior that has been difficult for you to accept and change. This behavior can be either directly or indirectly related to your trauma. It can also be a behavior that you are either currently struggling to change or have already successfully changed. Fill in as many boxes as apply to your behavior. I have provided two samples below to get you started on this exercise. The last chart is for you to complete on your own.

Example 1

Pre-contemplation	My use of pornography does not hurt anyone.
Contemplation	Why does my spouse get so bent out of shape if I am not actually cheating on her? Just to get her off my back, I will attend marriage counseling.

Preparation	Okay, so now to get my wife and the marriage counselor off my back, I will put blocks on all of my devices and turn over all log-in information to my spouse. I will also get a spiritual accountability partner.
Change	I have not viewed pornography for a week.
(Relapse)	I received a random email link. I wasn't sure what the link was about, so of course I opened it.
Maintenance	I have not viewed pornography for six months. I now automatically delete all emails that I do not recognize. My marriage is not perfect, but my wife is no longer on my case, and our sex life has actually improved (which I never thought would happen). Sometimes I still crave pornography, but now I have better coping skills and more transparent accountability.

Example 2

Pre-contemplation	People say I overreact when I don't get my way. I say that other people really tick me off on purpose.
Contemplation	My boss made me take an anger management class. For the third time. And he also said that this would be the last time. Okay, so maybe I do overreact more than most people. I don't know why I do this.
Preparation	I have decided to go to counseling. I have learned a lot about where my overreactions come from. I still have so much anger from the abuse. Not only am I learning new insights, I am also learning some really good coping skills.
Change	Today at work I had a chance to apply some of my new coping skills! I have not had a major blow-up in three months.
(Relapse)	Today at home I had another chance to apply some of my counseling skills. Unfortunately, I didn't use them. Got into a huge argument with my husband. Over absolutely nothing.
Maintenance	I still get more frustrated than most people. But now I am much more aware of my triggers, and I am getting better at using my coping skills. And when I catch myself overreacting, I also know how to repair the damage as quickly as possible and get back on track.

Your turn!

Pre-contemplation	
Contemplation	
Preparation	
Change	
(Relapse)	
Maintenance	

Congratulations, you have just learned the steps of long-term change! Perhaps the most important message from this lesson is that the only true changes we make are the changes that we have learned to maintain. If we want a garden of vegetables, it's not enough to think about planting the garden, it's not enough to get ready to plant the garden, and it's not even enough to plant the garden. If you want vegetables, you have to maintain that garden long after it's been planted! All of these principles apply to the garden of life.

OVERCOMING BLIND SPOTS

So far in this chapter, we have further developed the themes of awareness, acceptance, and action. We have learned that we cannot accept difficult facts or make difficult changes until we first overcome our *blind spots* (denial and pre-contemplation). By definition, we cannot see our blind spots on our own—we need help from others to kindly, gently point them out. We have also learned other roadblocks to acceptance (anger, bargaining, depression), and have further learned that no action is lasting until we have found ways to *maintain* that change. And finally, we have also learned that acceptance is often a prerequisite for action. In other words, we won't be motivated to change a problem if we haven't first accepted that it is indeed a problem!

But how do we get from acceptance to action? How do we accept that something really is a problem? And how do we start to change something once we have agreed that it is problematic? The next exercise will help answer these questions.

Moving from Acceptance to Action

Look at the blank chart that follows. Read through all the directions first, look at the sample, and then you can try filling out the chart on your own.

First, identify a behavior that you would like to evaluate in more detail. Describe this action in as much detail as you need. Then move to the next two rows. These boxes will help you *accept* whether this is a problem behavior. List all of the positive results that you can think of. Then list all of the negative results you can think of. Sometimes it is also helpful to distinguish between *short-term positives* versus *long-term positives*, as well as between *short-term negatives* and *long-term negatives*.

Now take a step back and look at the rows describing the results of your behavior. Are there more positives than negatives? Are there more negatives than positives? Remember that this is not just about numbers. Sometimes just one long-term negative consequence can far outweigh many positive short-term consequences. In the final analysis, are the negative results worth it? Or are there enough negative results to make this a problem behavior?

In short, these boxes have just helped you with acceptance.

But now how do you change the problem behavior? Well, let's take a look at the next two rows. These boxes are all about what preceded the behavior. The first of these two boxes is specifically about *external triggers*. External triggers answer questions such as: What? When? Who? Where? For example, *What was I doing before the behavior happened? When was this going on? Who was I with? Where was I?* The next box is about *internal triggers*. Internal triggers answer questions like: *What was going through my mind before the behavior happened? What was I feeling emotionally? What was I feeling physically?*

Guess what? Everything you just identified in these two boxes are called triggers! One of the keys to changing behavior is learning to identify, avoid, eliminate, or manage our triggers.

Let's check out a sample exercise first. And then it will be your turn.

Problem behavior	Overeating when I'm really stressed.
Positive results	Short term: I love to eat. I feel instant relief. Long term: Um, I can't really think of any.
Negative results	Short term: Immediately after overeating, I start to feel nauseous, and then I can't sleep. Long term: I gain weight. Then I have body image issues. And my clothes don't fit.
ACCEPTANCE	Based on these results, is this behavior worth it? Why or why not? Based on these results, this behavior causes more problems than it solves. While there are short-term benefits (I feel better in the moment), there are no long-term benefits. In addition, the negative consequences are both short term and long term.
External triggers	Who: When I am alone. What: Watching TV. When: After a stressful day of work. Where: In my bedroom. What are my main external triggers? My main external triggers seem to be when I am alone after a stressful day of work. If I either have a good day at work or I spend time with my husband processing the day, then I am much less likely to overeat.
Internal triggers	Feelings: Stressed. Overwhelmed. Worried. Anxious. Sensations: My muscles start to tense. My head hurts. Thoughts: I start to fantasize about my favorite junk food. What are my main internal triggers? Fantasizing about my favorite junk food is my main trigger. There are other times when I feel stressed and overwhelmed, or my head hurts and my muscles tense, but I do not actually overeat.
ACTION	How can I avoid, eliminate, or manage my triggers? My job is sometimes really stressful, but that's not really a trigger I can remove right now, because that would cause even more stress! However, some of these other triggers can definitely be managed or replaced by finding other ways to unwind after a stressful day at work. For example, instead of isolating in my bedroom and watching TV while fantasizing about junk food, I could go on a walk with my husband and process my day.

Problem behavior	
Positive results	Short term: Long term:
Negative results	Short term: Long term:
ACCEPTANCE	Based on these results, is this behavior worth it? Why or why not?
External triggers	Who: What: When: Where: What are my main external triggers?
Internal triggers	Feelings: Sensations: Thoughts: What are my main internal triggers?

ACTION	How can I avoid, eliminate, or manage my triggers?

Congratulations! You have just learned to accept *and* change problem behaviors in one simple chart. First, you learned to accept a problem behavior by identifying both the positive and the negative results of that behavior. Sometimes it's difficult to accept a behavior as a problem until we first see that the negative results outweigh the positive results. Next, you learned to change this problem behavior by identifying both the external and the internal triggers. As we learned, one of the quickest ways to change a problem behavior is to start avoiding, eliminating, or managing the triggers that lead up to it.

THE LAST WORD

In this chapter, we have seen that awareness, acceptance, and action are processes that take time and unfold gradually. We have also seen that the main obstacles to all three processes are blind spots. Our blind spots not only get in the way of awareness, they obstruct both acceptance and action as well.

The blind spot that gets in the way of acceptance is often called denial, while the blind spot that gets in the way of action is often called pre-contemplation. Don't worry about the terms, since they all refer to the same basic concept: We need to be brave enough to examine our blind spots (with help) so that we can move forward with both acceptance and action.

We have learned that anger, bargaining, and depression can pose additional roadblocks to acceptance. We have also seen that change is not complete if we just settle for contemplation, preparation, or even initial action. Change needs to be maintained!

And finally, we also learned a simple shortcut to help us move through the stages of acceptance and change. First, we learned to compare and contrast the positive and negative results of our behaviors to help us determine if they are problematic. This helps us with acceptance. Second, we learned to identify both the external and the internal triggers of our problem behavior. Learning to avoid, eliminate, or manage triggers is one of the quickest ways to jump-start a change in a problem behavior. The rest of this workbook will focus on specific skills for taking action in your life—and maintaining those changes.

CHAPTER 3

Restoring Balance with Better Coping

Remember the special formula for applied mindfulness?

applied mindfulness = awareness + acceptance + action

In non-math terms, this formula means we need to become more aware of what's happening in the moment. Then we need to become more accepting of what's happening in the moment. And then, once we are both more aware and more accepting, we are in a much better position to finally take action, that is, to deal with the situation.

When we experience trauma, however, we are not using the part of our brain that guides us through awareness, acceptance, and action. We are using a different part of the brain, one that is more concerned about our immediate survival. This part causes us to alter awareness, activate judgments, and jump straight to action as soon as possible. But there are only three main options for action with this part of the brain: fight, flight, or freeze.

The *fight* response means we become hostile or belligerent (whether physically, emotionally, or verbally). The *flight* response means we either physically leave or emotionally avoid a situation. And the *freeze* response means we just shut down altogether. An extreme example of the freeze response is fainting.

Many trauma survivors have been in situations in which it was not safe to fight back or to escape. That's precisely why they learned to freeze—and then escape in their own minds. This is a process that psychologists call *dissociation*. Dissociation is a combination of the freeze and flight response; this happens when you *mentally* freeze and then *mentally* escape, even if your body is still fully functioning and fully present in the situation.

All of these responses to danger or crisis are extremely helpful when we are experiencing a traumatic situation. Awareness is altered because you need to focus only on survival. Judgments are activated because you need to make quick, snappy decisions about life-or-death matters. Finally, you certainly do not have the luxury of consulting with a panel of experts on the best course of action. That's why your brain limits your choices to the three options most likely to help you survive: fight, flight, or freeze (which, as we saw, includes dissociation).

But here's the glitch: When we have been traumatized enough, we learn to execute these responses to everything in life—even if we are not in immediate danger or crisis. In other words, our brain *overlearns* these responses. Do you see the problem with that? Let's assume your coworker responds to you in a tone that you did not expect. Now let's assume that your awareness is altered (you only notice her stressed tone, not her baggy eyes from not sleeping last night) and that your judgments are activated instead of acceptance ("I can't believe I have to work with scum who gives me no respect!") and so you jump straight to fight, flight, or freeze. I will let your own imagination take over from there. But here's my point: Are you off to a good start at work? Did your trauma response just make things better—or a whole lot worse?

Remember that DBT is all about restoring balance? DBT has an entire set of skills called *distress tolerance* that are designed to provide temporary quick fixes to help us speedily restore balance in the moment, when we are triggered. In other words, the purpose of these skills is to give us alternatives to replace our instinctive fight-flight-freeze reactions and to get us back into our Balanced Mind as soon as possible.

One of my favorite definitions of distress tolerance is "how to survive the moment without making it worse." In short, distress tolerance is all about healthier and more effective ways of coping—as opposed to unhealthy or ineffective coping, in which you hurt yourself, hurt someone else, or make the problem worse than it already is. Another definition of distress tolerance that I really like is "turning unbearable pain into bearable pain." Notice that distress tolerance does not take away pain—but it does help you deal with painful situations in ways that do not cause the pain to become worse.

Ultimately, distress tolerance skills will help you with both acceptance and action. That's why the first distress tolerance skill you will learn is called *extreme acceptance*. As you will see, extreme acceptance is a special kind of acceptance that we need to apply to both trauma and its consequences. After you learn about extreme acceptance, you will next learn a series of coping skills that will help you take action—in other words, to react in more effective ways. Notice that effective coping involves both acceptance and action. This is another one of the great balancing acts of DBT!

FIGHT, FLIGHT, FREEZE

When you are triggered, what are your automatic reactions? Think of the fight, flight, and freeze responses we just learned about. How can these reactions make the situation even worse for you? I will provide some sample responses for you. And then it's your turn!

Fight	Example	When someone cuts me off in traffic, I lay on the horn and tailgate to teach them a lesson.
	Consequences	I have just made road conditions more hazardous for everyone, including myself.
Flight	Example	When I get in a big tiff with my wife, I take off in my car for the rest of the day, without telling her where I am.
	Consequences	The initial tiff does not get resolved. Even worse, when I come back home, we end up arguing even more—like about where I was—than whatever the original argument was about!
Freeze	Example	When I argue with my husband, I shut down and withdraw. My face becomes an emotional blank slate, and I tell him that everything's okay.
	Consequences	The initial argument does not get resolved. Even worse, my husband gets so ticked off that he leaves the house in a huff, which triggers even more feelings of abandonment in me.
Freeze + Flight (Dissociation)	Example	Whenever I'm at a meeting and my boss is wearing the same cologne as my abusive ex-boyfriend, I immediately check out and do not hear a word he is saying, even though I smile and nod and pretend I'm listening.
	Consequences	I have no recollection of the meeting. Which is a problem, because sometimes I end up agreeing to take on commitments that I cannot meet!

Now it's your turn. Think of recent instances when you were triggered and your automatic reactions kicked in. Then consider the consequences of those actions.

Fight	Example	
	Consequences	
Flight	Example	
	Consequences	
Freeze	Example	
	Consequences	
Freeze + Flight (Dissociation)	Example	
	Consequences	

EXTREME ACCEPTANCE

Not everything that happens to us in life is something we signed up for. There are some things in our past that we desperately wish had never happened to us. There are things in the present that we desperately wish we could change. In fact, there are even people whom we desperately wish we could change.

Extreme acceptance means accepting something that you emphatically do not like. Extreme acceptance does not mean that you approve of or agree with the situation—but it does mean that you will acknowledge and embrace the situation anyway. Extreme acceptance is the exact opposite of denial. As we learned in a previous chapter, denial is adaptive when we are still in shock and the brain needs to protect us from information that we cannot handle yet. But denial is no longer adaptive when we constantly have blinders on that prevent us from seeing reality how it really is. Long-term, ongoing denial is basically when we lie to ourselves—and then believe our own lie. Extreme acceptance, in contrast, means we see reality exactly how it is—no better and no worse.

Why should we learn to practice extreme acceptance? Well, here are a few reasons to consider. First, just because you deny reality does not mean that problems go away. In fact, the opposite is true: The more we make an ongoing habit of denying reality, the worse our problems get—not better!

Another reason to practice extreme acceptance is because pain cannot be avoided anyway. Pain is simply a fact of life. We all have pain. A baby's first emotional response to life is to cry. Why? Because coming into this world is painful—just ask the mother! And even death is sometimes painful. And then there's plenty of pain in between. So in short, it's not possible to avoid all that pain, no matter how hard we try.

A third reason to practice extreme acceptance is because of something we have started to learn: We must accept reality before we can change it. Accepting reality is indeed painful, because we are becoming more aware of painful things that we would prefer to ignore. But eventually, extreme acceptance leads to peace and freedom. Why? Because extreme acceptance puts us in a better position to deal with reality (Linehan 2015).

Since extreme acceptance can be such a difficult idea to grasp, here are two formulas that help me understand this concept better:

$$\text{pain} + \text{extreme acceptance} = \text{healing}$$

$$\text{pain} - \text{extreme acceptance} = \text{suffering}$$

There are several important lessons we can learn from these two simple formulas. I apologize ahead of time if an example from algebra will be triggering, but you can think of these two equations this way: Pain is the constant, while acceptance is the variable. As we have already seen, pain is a given: Both of these equations include pain. However, our response to pain is what determines the outcome of this equation. If we demonstrate extreme acceptance of the pain, we are now on the path to healing. Of course, as we have already seen, the path to healing can itself be painful…but at the very least, things will eventually start to get better. But when we do not practice extreme acceptance, that pain only gets worse. When pain gets worse instead of better, we experience suffering rather than healing.

Something else we can learn from these two formulas is that *pain is required but suffering is optional.* Let me explain what I mean by this statement. First of all, I do not mean that everything you have suffered in your life is your fault. However, now that you are learning new skills and new insights in this workbook, the pain in your life does not have to keep piling up or getting worse. By demonstrating extreme acceptance, you really can start to turn the tide on your suffering. You can switch from the path that leads to suffering to the path that leads to healing. Both paths will still have pain. But the pain on the healing path is bearable, while the pain on the suffering path is not. And that's an important difference!

Something that helps us better accept pain is understanding how much we need it. Yes, you heard me correctly. Let's use a physical example to explain what I mean. Pain is obviously a very uncomfortable experience—and that's precisely why it is such an important wake-up call. Pain is a signal that something is wrong. If our mind did not send us such a loud, clear message, we might not get it.

Even in a physical sense, pain allows us to heal, learn, and grow from our experiences. Think about it: You probably would not have survived childhood without it. There are indeed children who do not physically experience pain, and they actually have really high mortality rates. Why? Because when they are injured, they have no signal from their brain telling them to stop, get help, or pursue a different course of action. I for one would never have survived childhood without pain—in fact, I barely survived with it! The same principles apply to us emotionally: We need emotional pain to heal, learn, and grow. The more we can understand the benefits of pain, the easier it becomes to demonstrate extreme acceptance. And since pain is a signal, the more we listen to it, the less it has to scream at us to get our attention.

There are three basic scenarios in which we need to practice extreme acceptance:

1. Situations from the past that cannot be changed

2. Situations from the present that cannot be changed

3. Situations from the present that can be changed

Perhaps you were raped as a child. That's an example of a situation from the past that cannot be changed. As much as you wish it did not happen, that does not change the fact that it did happen. Or perhaps you have some sort of permanent disability. That is an example of a situation from the present that also cannot be changed. As much as you wish you did not have the disability, that will not change the fact that you have it.

But sometimes there are situations from the present that *can* be changed. For example, perhaps you are involved in an abusive relationship. Perhaps you have tried to change your abusive partner but you could not. But there's still another option that perhaps you have ignored: Get out of the relationship!

In all three cases, extreme acceptance is not easy (to say the least). However, as we have already seen, failing to demonstrate extreme acceptance would not help any of these scenarios. Pain would only become suffering. Extreme acceptance is precisely what we need in order to deal with each of these scenarios. Therefore, extreme acceptance is emphatically not a passive process, although at times it may seem that way. As we have seen, some situations in life can be changed while others cannot. Regardless, extreme acceptance always provides an opportunity to change what can be changed. For example, you cannot change the fact that you were raped—but you can change how you decide to relate to men now. You cannot change the fact that you have a disability, but you can decide to optimize your life regardless of the disability—and perhaps even because of the disability! And maybe you cannot change an abusive partner—but you can decide whether you remain in that relationship.

Barriers to Extreme Acceptance

Here are some signs that you might not be demonstrating extreme acceptance about something important in your life. Which of these barriers to acceptance can you relate to? Provide a personal example for as many of these barriers that apply to you. As you complete this exercise, think about how these forms of nonacceptance make the situation worse instead of better.

Lying: _____

_____

_____

_____

_____

_____

_____

Denial: _____

_____

_____

_____

_____

_____

_____

_____

Blaming: _____

_____

_____

_____

_____

_____

_____

Justifying: _____

_____

_____

_____

_____

_____

_____

_____

Avoidance: _____

_____

_____

_____

_____

_____

_____

_____

Distraction: _____

_____

_____

_____

_____

_____

_____

_____

Minimizing: _____

_____

_____

_____

_____

_____

_____

Rationalizing: _____

_____

_____

_____

_____

_____

_____

Manipulating: _____

_____

_____

_____

_____

_____

_____

Making excuses: _____

_____

_____

_____

_____

_____

_____

Let's Get Visual

Imagine that it is 2:00 a.m. and your precious newborn baby is screaming her head off. You have several options. First you decide to completely ignore the baby. Next you decide to scream back at the baby. Finally you decide to embrace the baby.

Do you see how the first two responses are forms of nonacceptance? Do you see how ignoring the baby or screaming at the baby will not help the situation—and will certainly not help the baby? Do you see how the most effective and efficient way of calming the baby—not to mention the healthiest—would be to simply embrace the baby?

How does this analogy apply to life in general? Do I ever ignore life? Do I ever scream at life? How so?

_____

_____

_____

_____

_____

_____

_____

_____

_____

How does this analogy relate to the concept of extreme acceptance? How is embracing life (even when it is uncomfortable) the best way of dealing with life?

_____

_____

_____

_____

_____

_____

_____

_____

Let's Get Philosophical

Read this quote from Dr. M. Scott Peck (1978, 15).

> "Life is difficult. This is a great truth, one of the greatest truths. It is a great truth because once we truly see this truth, we transcend it. Once we truly know that life is difficult—once we truly understand and accept it—then life is no longer difficult. Because once it is accepted, the fact that life is difficult no longer matters."

How does this paragraph relate to extreme acceptance?

_____

_____

_____

_____

_____

_____

_____

Read this quote from Dr. Viktor Frankl (1984, 51).

"When we are no longer able to change a situation, we are challenged to change ourselves."

How does this line relate to extreme acceptance?

_____

_____

_____

_____

_____

_____

_____

Take a look at the famous Serenity Prayer.

"God, grant me the serenity to accept the things I cannot change, the courage to change the things I can, and the wisdom to know the difference."

How is this prayer another example of extreme acceptance?

_____

_____

_____

_____

_____

_____

_____

So far, the concept of extreme acceptance may seem somewhat abstract and theoretical. So let's make this concept as concrete and practical as possible with real-life examples.

Accepting Life: The Good, Bad, and Ugly

Think of three areas in your life that need to be accepted in order for you to continue your healing journey. Try to think of one example from the past (which, by definition, cannot be changed). Then think of at least two examples from the present: at least one situation that can be changed and at least one that cannot.

As you complete this exercise, ask yourself: *How does extreme acceptance put me in a better position to either deal with or heal from this situation? How does not accepting the situation make things even worse?* The first chart is a sample. And then it's your turn!

Something from the past:	My grandfather molested me when I was child.
Something from the present that cannot be changed:	My grandfather will be at the family reunion.
Something from the present that can be changed:	I want to go to the family reunion. But I can decide whether to interact with my grandfather. I can also leave whenever I feel uncomfortable.

Something from the past:	
Something from the present that cannot be changed:	
Something from the present that can be changed:	

So far in this chapter, we have learned about extreme acceptance. It is easy to accept something we like. However, it is much more difficult to accept something we do *not* like. And that is precisely why extreme acceptance is so extreme! Extreme acceptance does not mean that we like a situation; it simply means that we are willing to face it and deal with it anyway. When we do not practice extreme acceptance, pain becomes suffering; when we do practice extreme acceptance, we are on the path to healing. Extreme acceptance is the foundation for effective coping…which is the topic of the next lesson.

THE COPING PANTHEON

A formula we have seen repeatedly in this workbook is:

applied mindfulness = awareness + acceptance + action

As we have already learned, awareness and acceptance can often transform our lives from unbearable to bearable, from unmanageable to manageable. Obviously, however, sometimes life requires additional action beyond awareness and acceptance. But here's the good news: First, awareness and acceptance are already forms of action. Second, awareness and acceptance are precisely the foundation we need in order to respond to life with specific, concrete behaviors. Otherwise, we are just back to our old ineffective habits and impulsive reactions that only make matters worse.

Now that we have laid this foundation of awareness and acceptance, the rest of this workbook will focus on specific, concrete behaviors. In this lesson, we will introduce some basic, short-term strategies we can use to cope in the moment and return to our Balanced Mind.

Remember all those ways our mind can get off balance? Sometimes our Thinking Mind is in overdrive, and we can't stop worrying or obsessing. Sometimes our Thinking Mind isn't working enough—and we make reactive or impulsive decisions. Sometimes our Feeling Mind is in overdrive, which makes us feel overwhelmed or out of control. And sometime our Feeling Mind isn't working enough—which makes us feel numb, empty, or even dead.

People do many things when either their Thinking Mind or Feeling Mind is off balance. Some people use drugs. Some people rage. Some people engage in self-harm. Some people keep making the same mistakes over and over again. Perhaps you can relate to some of these patterns. Regardless, they all have the same outcome: Although many of these reactions may help you feel better in the moment—or at the very least provide some sort of temporary relief—they all make things even worse in the long haul. Just think about it: How could drugs, rage, self-harm, or knee-jerk reactions really help you turn your life around? You already know the answer to that!

Therefore, the entire purpose of all the coping skills in this chapter is to get you back into your Balanced Mind as efficiently and effectively as possible without incurring further collateral damage. You will achieve this by learning alternative behaviors to replace the behaviors you would normally engage in.

As you learn each of these new coping skills, here are a few points to keep in mind: First, *practice makes prepared—not perfect*. The more you practice these skills, the more prepared you will feel to face your triggers. Don't worry about perfection—save that for a different lifetime.

Second, the time to practice these skills is when you are *not* in crisis. Please do not wait for a crisis situation to try out a new coping skill!

Third, you need to integrate as many of these coping skills into your normal daily routine as possible. These coping skills will have both a preventive and a rehabilitative effect. In other words, the more your coping skills become part of your normal lifestyle, the less you will feel triggered in the first place—and the better you will deal with the triggers when they do happen.

Fourth, it is important to remember that all of these skills work for someone—but none of these skills works for everyone. The key is to figure out which of these coping skills will work for *you*!

So let's get started already.

Pros and Cons

Pros and cons is the first coping skill in this list, because this is the skill that helps us realize that we need to cope in the first place. This skill is especially useful when we would much rather do something impulsive (an *action urge*), as opposed to coping.

It is well documented that previous trauma makes us more impulsive. In one study of 412 people with trauma histories, researchers identified the importance of replacing sensation-seeking tendencies—especially when triggered by negative emotions—with more effective forms of coping (Contractor et al. 2016).

So the next time you feel like doing something impulsive, it may be helpful to think through the pros and cons of engaging in your *action urge* (in other words, what you feel like doing in the moment); and then think through the pros and cons of instead choosing one of the coping strategies described in this book; and then think about which of the two options would be best for you in the long term.

It is especially helpful to ask yourself the following questions: *Which option will help me get back into my Balanced Mind as soon as possible? Which options will help me best meet my long-term goals?*

	Pros	Cons
Action Urge		
Coping Skill		

Half Smile

Research shows that changing our facial expressions can also change our mood (Linehan 2015). This works for a variety of negative emotions, including anger, anxiety, and depression. One of the best ways to change your facial expressions (and therefore your mood as well) is simply to smile—even if you don't feel like it. And if you can't smile all the way, then don't—just do a *half smile*! The goal here is simply to train your facial muscles to produce a more contented countenance, which in turn will help you feel more content in reality.

But the perks of smiling don't stop there: Smiling also influences the moods of others. In one study (Lynn 2011), waiters increased their tips by 140 percent—just by smiling! In fact, research even shows that smiles are the facial expressions people can recognize from the farthest distance (Frank 2016). In short, not only does smiling improve your own mood, it is also a great way to contagiously get *other* people in a better mood as well—which, in turn, will make your day even better!

Change the Temperature

Research shows that immersing your face in cold water has an immediate calming effect on the entire body (Neacsiu, Bohus, and Linehan 2015). Research also shows that feeling connected to someone and temperature are strongly linked (Vess 2012). For example, you will feel more connected to someone if you are holding a hot cup of tea!

In short, another way to influence your emotions is to shift your body temperature. So take a cold shower. Or take a hot shower. Or grab an ice cube. Or soak in some rays. Or drink a simmering hot beverage. Or drink an ice-cold beverage. You get the point!

Intense Exercise

Exercise releases natural chemicals in your brain that make you feel better. That's why another way to quickly shift your mood is through rigorous physical activity. In one study of eighty-one people with PTSD, all eighty-one participants received comprehensive trauma treatment, including individual counseling, group counseling, and appropriate medications (Rosenbaum, Sherrington, and Tiedemann 2015). However, only thirty-nine subjects participated in an exercise program. By the end of the study, the exercise group had less PTSD, less depression—and less waist!

There are many ways to exercise. You don't have to run marathons, become an Iron Man, get a gym membership, or buy lots of expensive equipment. It's completely okay to just go for a walk or ride your bike. But if that's too boring for you, here are some more options: Shoot some hoops. Lift some weights. Do some sit-ups, push-ups, or chin-ups. Cut the grass. Cut the neighbor's grass. Garden. Do a physical project around the house. There are many options for exercise besides surfing the web or playing fantasy football!

Controlled Breathing

Controlled breathing sends oxygen to your brain from your abdomen rather than from your chest. Breathing from your chest is one way to trigger or reinforce the fight-flight-freeze response we discussed earlier. However, breathing from your abdomen sends the signal to your brain that all is well, which in turn has a calming effect on your whole body.

Another good thing about breathing as a coping strategy is that it doesn't take any extra time, since it's something you have to do anyway. In one study of veterans from Iraq and Afghanistan, breathing exercises significantly reduced both PTSD and anxiety symptoms—even one year after the study ended (Seppälä et al. 2014).

Here's the basic pattern that most forms of controlled breathing follow:

1. Place one hand on your stomach.

2. Place the other hand on your chest.

3. Breathe in through your nose.

4. Breathe out through your mouth.

5. Exhale for twice as long as you inhale.

6. Make sure the hand on your chest remains still.

7. Observe the hand on your stomach rise and fall with your breathing cycle.

Muscle Relaxation

There are also many variations of *muscle relaxation*. However, all of the variations have one basic theme in common: learning to both tighten and relax your muscles. There are two reasons that such a simple exercise can be so helpful. First, it is helpful to simply become more aware of how our muscles feel when they are either tense or relaxed. Our body is constantly communicating to us, and often the body talks to us through our muscles. So when our muscles are tight, that usually means we are stressed about something.

Second, learning to tighten and relax our muscles also teaches us that we have some control over how our muscles feel. For example, if we can deliberately tighten our muscles, that also means we can deliberately relax them—which then helps our entire system to relax. One study examined the effects of muscle relaxation on eighty women who had received hysterectomies. This study found that the forty patients who practiced muscle relaxation following the operation had lower stress, anxiety, and depression than the forty patients who only received the normal nursing care (Essa, Ismail, and Hassan 2017).

Here are two of my favorite forms of muscle relaxation:

METHOD A

1. Identify the major muscle groups in your body where you feel the most tension when stressed.

2. Tighten that muscle as hard as you can for three seconds. Then release. Then repeat the entire step.

3. Repeat step 2 with the parallel muscle from the other side of your body (if applicable).

4. Repeat steps 2 and 3 with all of the muscle groups identified in step 1.

METHOD B

1. Tighten all of the major muscle groups in your entire body.

2. Imagine a gentle waterfall landing first on your head, and then slowly cascading through your entire body, all the way down to your toes.

3. Starting with your head, relax each muscle group as the cascade passes through your body.

Making Comparisons

Sometimes we feel like we are the only one with problems or that our problems are much worse than everyone else's. That's when it is sometimes helpful to make some realistic comparisons to balance out our thinking. In one study of seventy people with spinal cord injuries, those who were able to compare themselves to others who were worse off had more constructive coping than those who did not make these comparisons (Buunk, Buunk, Zurriaga, and González 2007).

Here are some examples of comparisons that some people find helpful:

- Think of someone who is worse off than you are.

- Think of how your situation could hypothetically be worse than it is.

- Think of a time in the past when things were even more difficult than they are now.

- Think of all the progress you have made so far.

Keep in mind that even though the technique of *making comparisons* can be very effective for some people, it does not work for everyone, for several reasons. For example, some people feel it is too negative to compare someone else's misery to their own. Other people feel this technique sends an invalidating message: "Don't be such a wimp, when other people have it worse." In addition, some people are so sensitive that just thinking about someone else's suffering makes their own suffering even worse. And still others feel that making comparisons can be used as grounds for justification: "Well, at least I wasn't as drunk as she was!" If any of these scenarios apply to you, stayed tuned for the next coping skill...

Counting Blessings

For people who do not benefit from the making comparisons technique, there is a great alternative called *counting blessings*. Instead of coping by reframing the negatives, counting blessings works by focusing on the positives: *What is going well for me? What can I be thankful for? How have I been blessed? What gifts, strengths, and talents do I have? Who are my best friends and biggest supporters?*

One group of researchers studied the role of gratitude in 182 college women with trauma histories. These researchers found that *thankful* college students had fewer PTSD symptoms, *regardless* of the severity of the trauma, extent of the previous trauma history, or amount of time elapsed since the trauma occurred (Vernon, Dillon, and Steiner 2009).

Finding Humor

Humor is another great way to quickly shift your mood. Perhaps you have heard the adage that "laughter is the best medicine." This is a very old concept, going all the way back to the ancient Hebrews. For example, the Hebrew Bible says: "A merry heart does good, like a medicine" (Prov. 17:22). Indeed, modern research supports this claim. For example, one study found that having a good sense of humor was linked to lower burnout and trauma symptoms in 179 firefighters (Sliter, Kale, and Yuan 2014).

So it's worth figuring out: What makes you laugh? What do you think is funny? Think of your favorite comedian. Think of a funny joke. Think of a really funny movie. Think of your funniest memory. Think of a friend who has a great sense of humor. Think of a YouTube video that makes you laugh, no matter how many times you see it. In short, create a "funny bank" that you can draw from, whenever you need to. In addition, try to find the humor in even the worst of situations. If you look hard enough, there's almost always a funny side to life!

Container

Sometimes we have certain words, worries, images, or memories go through our mind, and we wish they wouldn't. Sometimes the more we tell ourselves not to think about them, the more we think about them! Have you ever argued with someone about whether or not you were arguing? What happened when you tried to convince the other person that you weren't arguing? You continued to argue, of course!

It's the same principle with your thoughts: Instead of trying to think about not thinking about something, sometimes you just need to find a way to stop thinking about something altogether. One great way of doing that is to image some kind of *container*. This could be a safe, a trunk, a vault, or any other kind of container. Next, take whatever words, worries, images, or memories you don't want to think about and lock them up in that container! And since only you have the key, you do not have to unlock your container until you are ready.

Memorization

Containing a disturbing or distressful thought is indeed a great start, but how do you replace that thought with a different one so that you don't go back to the original one? That's where *memorization* comes in handy. Once you have contained a problem thought, default to repeating something over and over again that you already know by memory. This could be a favorite song, poem, prayer, quote, expression, saying—anything that can be turned into what I call a "mantra for the moment."

In one study of 182 women, the participants who regularly memorized the Koran demonstrated less anxiety and depression and better sleep and social function than those who did not (Kimiaee, Khademian, and Farhadi 2012).

Helping Others

The original creators of the 12 steps learned that helping others maintain sobriety was the best way for them to maintain their own sobriety—and that's precisely why the twelfth step is all about *helping others* (Alcoholics Anonymous 2002).

There are many studies suggesting that helping others can be a great way of helping ourselves. In fact, one author reviewed almost twenty-five thousand articles on volunteering. This researcher found that people who volunteer tend to have better mental health, physical health, life satisfaction, social interaction, coping, and even longevity (Casiday 2015).

More and more research shows that volunteering can especially help people heal from trauma symptoms. One study of 356 veterans returning from Iraq and Afghanistan found that participating in a national civic service significantly improved many aspects of physical, mental, and social health—including reduction in both depression and PTSD (Matthieu, Lawrence, and Robertson-Blackmore 2017).

Think of ways that you could help someone else that would also provide you with a sense of purpose, fulfillment, satisfaction, or relief. This can be as simple as volunteering at a soup kitchen, babysitting someone's children, or mowing the neighbor's lawn.

Some people, however, are people-pleasers in unhealthy ways, meaning that they already focus too much on helping other people meet their needs, at the expense of their own. In fact, some people tend to help others as an escape from dealing with their own problems, or they only feel like they have any worth when they are helping needy people. If you can relate to this description, then helping others may not be the best coping skill for you. But don't worry—there are plenty of other options to choose from.

Self-Care

Remember that DBT is all about balance? That's why we need to balance helping others with taking care of ourselves. Both can be really effective ways of coping—but only with the proper balance!

There are many ways of practicing *self-care*. Sometimes the first step in improving self-care is learning to practice basic habits of health and hygiene: eating well, sleeping enough, grooming ourselves, and so forth. The next step in self-care is learning to treat, pamper, and nurture ourselves—without feeling guilty. This will be different for everyone. For some people, this might be taking a nice long bubble bath. For others, it might be splurging on a well-deserved cup of gourmet coffee. Ironically, research shows that counselors are often not very good at practicing self-care themselves (Figley 2002). (Note to self: Practice what you preach, Kirby!)

Looking Back

When we are in a funk, we tend to make things more permanent than they really are. We tend to think our problems were always this bad and will always be this bad. In other words, we take our current situation and project it both backward and forward in time. That's why one way of coping in the present is to remember and reflect on positive memories from the past.

Use this opportunity to remind yourself that things have not always been as bad as they seem right now. Recall good times from the past that can give you the strength, encouragement, and motivation to get through the present. In one study of twenty-six older adults with moderate to severe depression, reminiscing about positive events from the past significantly reduced their symptoms (Watt and Cappeliez 2010). In fact, in one of the groups, 100 percent of the participants continued to demonstrate clinical improvement three months after the experiment ended!

Looking Forward

Life would be unbearable at times without hope. One way to cope in the present is to think ahead to when the current situation will be over or be better. Make a list of your goals, plans, dreams, ambitions, and aspirations. Think about how what you are going through now is helping to prepare you for better things down the road. Look for the light at the end of the tunnel. Remind yourself: *This too shall pass!*

There is a lot of research on the benefits of hope. In one study of 164 veterans with PTSD, higher levels of hope were associated with less depression and less trauma symptoms (Gilman, Schumm, and Chard 2012).

One Thing at a Time

Sometimes life becomes overwhelming when we start to think about all of our problems at once. That's when it's helpful to hit the pause button, take a step back, and choose just one thing to focus on. If necessary, make a list of everything you need to get done, rank these tasks in the order of importance, and then focus on *one thing at a time.*

There are decades of research indicating that learning to pay attention to just one thing at a time—in other words, mindfulness—helps improve just about every human symptom, whether physiological or psychological, including PTSD (Kearney et al. 2011, among hundreds of examples).

Mini Vacation

Something else we can do when everything starts to pile up is to simply take a temporary break from things—and then return when we are ready. There are many ways to take a *mini vacation.* Go for a walk. Take a bath. Go out to eat. Watch a movie. Go for a drive. Take a coffee break. Cook your favorite meal. The goal here is not to avoid your problems but simply to take the time you need so that you can get back in the game as soon as you are ready.

One study found that even people who experienced major life-altering events (such as spinal cord injuries or chronic illness) improved their coping and made their immediate life circumstances more bearable by learning to take mini vacations (Hutchinson et al. 2003).

Cheerleading

In a previous chapter, we talked about judgments. As you may recall, judgments come from the negative messages we hear from others. When other people say negative things to us enough times, eventually we start to make those messages our own negative self-talk. Sometimes what we desperately need is for someone else to say something nice or positive to counteract those judgments running through our heads. And that's great when that happens. But what do we do when there is no one around in the moment to be our cheerleader? That's precisely when we need to be our own cheerleader!

This skill is about learning to provide ourselves with the positive self-talk that we need to compete with our negative self-talk. In this case, cheerleading does not mean putting on a small skirt and jumping up and down with pom-poms—but it does mean giving yourself a pep talk! How effective is cheerleading? Well, research suggests that positive self-talk will even improve your dart-throwing accuracy (Van Raalte et al. 1995). 'Nuff said…

Journaling

Another way of coping is through any sort of *written expression*—and it doesn't even have to be words! Some of my clients love to write poetry (and I love to read their poems). And some of my clients love to draw (and I love to see their drawings). Regardless, finding creative ways to express our thoughts and feelings in written form can be very therapeutic.

In one study of U.S. veterans who had spent time in Afghanistan and Iraq, expressive writing resulted in less PTSD, anger, and physical complaints compared to veterans who did not write at all. In fact, veterans who wrote expressively even experienced better reintegration and social support than their peers (Sayer et al. 2015). Not sure if you have noticed this or not, but I have been making you do plenty of journaling in this workbook! You can thank me later…

Enjoyable Activities

What's something you really enjoy doing that costs very little money—or no money at all? Sipping a cup of coffee? Watching the sunset? Walking your dog? Getting comfy with a good book? Taking a shower? If you want to cope well with life, you need to do at least one enjoyable activity per day!

In one study, people who participated in more frequent enjoyable activities reported more positive emotions, life satisfaction, and social support as well as less depression, blood pressure, and stress hormones (Pressman et al. 2009) than those who did fewer enjoyable activities. Life is simply too short to be a workaholic all the time. Take time to enjoy life! (Another note to self: Practice what you preach, Kirby!)

Soothing with the Senses

Research shows that *mindfully engaging the five senses* (sight, sound, smell, taste, touch) can lower symptoms of depression, anxiety, and PTSD. For example, one study found that systematic exposure to certain aromas decreased symptoms of both anxiety and depression (Lemon 2004). Another study found that massage therapy significantly influenced brain chemistry. For example, massages decreased stress hormones (cortisol) while increasing neurotransmitters associated with positive emotions, such as dopamine and serotonin (Field et al. 2005).

Yet another study found that listening to music helped reduce anxiety—and even pain and fatigue—in terminally ill patients (Horne-Thompson and Grocke 2008). In fact, one study even found that music therapy could be more effective in treating depression than counseling (Castillo-Pérez et al. 2010)…but please do not tell your therapist that!

That's why another way to cope in the moment is to mindfully engage at least one of your five senses—and use that sense to focus on something that has a calming effect on you. You can mindfully gaze at something that is soothing to look at, or mindfully listen to something that calms you down. Perhaps you can mindfully absorb your favorite aroma or fragrance, or mindfully ingest your favorite flavor or ingredient. Or maybe you can mindfully relish a favorite tactile sensation (such as a comfy blanket or warm water streaming down your back). Some people even find it's helpful to create a Five-Senses Pouch, a way to easily and immediately engage all five senses at all times. For example, you might have perfume, candy, and a small stress ball in a zip-top baggie, along with a favorite picture or song on your phone, all within reach.

Ride the Wave

This coping skill is all about visualizing our intense emotions as a wave, and then learning to interact with that emotional wave the same way we would deal with a real wave. Consider this: If we are at the beach and a big wave is coming, we always have a couple of options. One option is to simply get out of the water, if we have enough time. But if that is not possible, another option is to just ride the wave. Yes, it will feel uncomfortable. Yes, we will feel like we are losing control. But what we do not want to do is fight the wave, which will only make matters worse!

When people panic at the beach, their first instinct is to control the wave by fighting it—kicking and thrashing. The only problem: We cannot control a wave, no matter how much we kick and thrash, but a wave can control us! In fact, the more we try to control a wave, the less control we actually have. And if a wave really controls us, we might even be completely knocked off balance and then get caught in the undertow. Which, trust me, is a really scary experience. Since I grew up in Connecticut, which has awful beaches, I have childhood memories of getting pulled under and dragged along the rocks and seaweed of the undertow!

All of these concepts apply to emotions. Sometimes if you notice an intense emotional wave coming, you can simply get out of the situation that is causing the wave. But if you cannot, then your next best option is to simply ride out the wave. Yes, you will feel uncomfortable. Yes, you will feel like you are losing some control. But just like a real wave, you cannot control emotions. And just like a real wave, the more you try to control emotions, the more the emotions will control you.

And just like people try to control a real wave by kicking and thrashing, people try to control their emotions through judgments. We say, "I should not feel this way," "This is stupid," "I hate depression." And if you judge your emotions too much, you just might end up in the emotional undertow, which will drag you through all kinds of emotional rocks and seaweed. Think about it: If you are angry, and you judge yourself for being angry, you will become angry at the anger, which just makes your anger problem even worse, not better! That's why it's always better to ride the wave than to fight the wave.

The same idea of learning to ride our emotional waves also applies to intense urges (such as craving a certain drug). That's why this same basic skill is sometimes called *urge surfing*. Research suggests that urge surfing can be an effective way to overcome strong cravings for alcohol, nicotine, and other drugs (Bowen and Marlatt 2009; Ostafin and Marlatt 2008).

Imagery

It's not always possible to cope by doing something specific. That's when *imagery* comes in handy. Imagery is all about visualizing something instead of actually doing it. Visualizing is more accessible and more portable than some of these other coping skills, because we can do it anywhere, anytime.

Think of some of the other coping skills we've been talking about, such as Self-Care, Enjoyable Activities, Mini Vacation, and Soothing with the Senses. In the event that you cannot actually implement these coping skills in the moment, would just visualizing them be helpful? In one study of 130 surgical patients, the participants who received guided imagery before, during, and following the operation experienced significantly less anxiety and pain—and required 50 percent less narcotic medications (Tusek, Church, and Fazio 2006)! So if visualizing a coping skill is just as effective or almost as effective as actually doing it, and you're not in a position to act on the coping skill, then imagery is for you.

Finding Purpose

Some situations in life seem so painful that no amount of physical *or* virtual coping will provide much relief. That's when it is necessary to practice *extreme acceptance*. Something that can make extreme acceptance a little easier to implement is to think about how your current suffering can be redeemed for a greater purpose. Learn to ask and answer questions such as the following:

What can I learn from this suffering that I could not have learned otherwise?

How can this suffering prepare me for something that nothing else could have prepared me for?

How can this suffering be used for good?

If these sorts of deep philosophical questions are difficult for you, consult with a spiritual leader, such as a pastor, priest, or rabbi.

Viktor Frankl was a Jewish psychiatrist who survived several different Nazi concentration camps during World II, including Auschwitz, where more than one million people died from brutal treatment, including starvation. Frankl later wrote a book called *Man's Search for Meaning* (1984) in which he described his experiences in the concentration camps. It is clear that Frankl inspired Marsha Linehan, the originator of DBT. Throughout his book, Frankl especially describes the coping skills that both he and others used to survive their hellish experiences. In fact, almost every single paragraph in his book makes reference to skills described in this chapter (as well as in other chapters). But as the title of his book implies, the most important coping skill Frankl references is *finding meaning (or purpose)* in suffering. Knowing that he was probably going to die anyway, Frankl decided against suicide and chose to use whatever time he had left in the camps to serve his fellow prisoners. According to Frankl, people who were able to find purpose in their suffering and maintain hope were much more likely to survive than those who did not.

Creating My Coping Card

Now that you have learned all of these different coping skills, you need to make a Coping Card. Here are the steps:

1. Write down as many specific ideas as you can think of for each of the forms of coping. You will probably end up with a long list. Remember that all of these skills work for someone, but none of these skills work for everyone. The point for now is simply to brainstorm—you aren't committing to doing every single idea you come up with. Having trouble starting? I've provided some examples.

Change the Temperature: *Drink a cold beverage and then take a hot shower after a stressful day at work.*

_____

_____

_____

_____

_____

_____

_____

Controlled Breathing: *Focus on my breathing every night before I go to sleep as a way to relax.*

_____

_____

_____

_____

_____

_____

_____

Making Comparisons: When I get discouraged about a recent relapse, I can think about how much progress I have made since I started learning DBT!

_____

_____

_____

_____

_____

_____

_____

_____

Counting Blessings: Make a gratitude list of everything that I am thankful for whenever I feel like giving up.

_____

_____

_____

_____

_____

_____

_____

_____

Pros and Cons: _____

_____

_____

_____

_____

_____

_____

Half Smile: _____

_____

_____

_____

_____

_____

_____

_____

Intense Exercise: _____

_____

_____

_____

_____

_____

_____

Muscle Relaxation: _____

_____

_____

_____

_____

_____

_____

Finding Humor: _____

_____

_____

_____

_____

_____

_____

Memorization: _____

_____

_____

_____

_____

_____

_____

Helping Others: _____

_____

_____

_____

_____

_____

_____

Self-Care: _____

_____

_____

_____

_____

_____

_____

_____

Looking Back: _____

_____

_____

_____

_____

_____

_____

Looking Forward: _____

_____

_____

_____

_____

_____

_____

_____

One Thing at a Time: _____

_____

_____

_____

_____

_____

_____

_____

Mini Vacation: _____

_____

_____

_____

_____

_____

_____

_____

Cheerleading: _____

_____

_____

_____

_____

_____

_____

Journaling: _____

_____

_____

_____

_____

_____

_____

Enjoyable Activities: _____

_____

_____

_____

_____

_____

_____

Soothing with the Senses: _____

_____

_____

_____

_____

_____

_____

Ride the Wave: _____

_____

_____

_____

_____

_____

_____

Imagery: _____

_____

_____

_____

_____

_____

_____

_____

Finding Purpose: _____

_____

_____

_____

_____

_____

_____

2. Go over what you wrote and pay special attention to specific activities that emerge in more than one category. For example, if you wrote "riding my bike" under Intense Exercise, Self-Care, Enjoyable Activities, and Mini Vacation, then you know you found a keeper! Put a star next to it.

3. Now review each item on your list, and cross out any coping skill that you think might not work or that you probably wouldn't actually use. You only want coping skills on your list that will consistently work for you. You don't want so many options that the list is overwhelming. But you also need enough options in case one coping skill is not possible.

4. Now let's create the actual Coping Card. There are many ways to do this. Back in the olden days when DBT was first created, people made actual cards with reminders of their coping skills. This is still a good way of doing it, which is why I'm asking you to fill out the chart below. Go back to your list and place a star next to each activity that you think will be the most effective for you most of the time. Write that activity in the second column.

Coping Skill	Specific Examples of When or How to Apply
Change the Temperature	
Controlled Breathing	
Making Comparisons	

Coping Skill	Specific Examples of When or How to Apply
Counting Blessings	
Pros and Cons	
Half Smile	
Intense Exercise	
Muscle Relaxation	
Finding Humor	
Memorization	
Helping Others	
Self-Care	
Looking Back	
Looking Forward	

Coping Skill	Specific Examples of When or How to Apply
One Thing at a Time	
Mini Vacation	
Cheerleading	
Journaling	
Enjoyable Activities	
Soothing with the Senses	
Ride the Wave	
Imagery	
Finding Purpose	

5. Incorporate as many coping skills into your daily routine as possible. Make these coping skills part of your lifestyle—your new normal. You can even combine your favorite coping skills for added effect. For example, I love to sip coffee while reading, or pray while riding my bicycle. Visualize the skills even when you can't use them. And don't forget: Practice makes prepared! Remember that your Coping Card is your temporary Balanced Mind. In other words, the Coping Card is what we need to resort to when we are not in our real Balanced Mind. That means your Coping Card needs to always be immediately accessible.

6. Share your Coping Card with your friends, your counselor, your mentor, your sponsor, your spouse, your spiritual guide, and other people within your support network. If other people know about your Coping Card, they will be able to provide you with moral support and accountability.

7. Revise your Coping Card as needed. Consider this a "living document" in both senses of the word. Not only will these coping skills be your lifeline, they will also continue to evolve over time, and you want to make sure your list is up to date with your current needs.

THE LAST WORD

Trauma activates our judgments and limits our options to fight, flight, and freeze. While these judgments and reactions are adaptive—and necessary—during periods of danger or crisis, they are ineffective ways of dealing with the rest of life. Distress tolerance skills were designed to replace unhelpful judgments with extreme acceptance and provide alternatives to fight, flight, and freeze, as well as other impulsive and destructive urges.

When it comes to coping skills, it is important to remember the following points: First, the time to learn these skills is when you are calm and stable; please don't wait for your next crisis to start practicing. Second, all of these skills work for some people, but none of these skills works for everyone. Be patient and figure out which of these skills work for you. Third, create some sort of physical or digital Coping Card to serve as your temporary Balanced Mind whenever you have lost your balance!

Finally, remember that coping skills are designed to be short-term solutions to get us back into the Balanced Mind as quickly as possible. In other words, these skills are all about coping in the moment, making the moment better, or, at the very least, not making the moment worse. While coping skills can certainly lead to significant long-term changes, coping skills alone will not change your thought patterns, your emotional climate, or how you relate to other people. For the rest of your toolbox, you need to keep reading!

CHAPTER 4

Restoring Balance with Thoughts

In the first chapter we learned about the three minds: the Thinking Mind, the Feeling Mind, and the Balanced Mind. Do you remember how both our thoughts and our feelings can get off balance when we are not using our Balanced Mind? Do you also remember that the purpose of the Balanced Mind is to notice, evaluate, regulate, and ultimately *balance* what we are thinking and feeling?

The entire point of this chapter is to use the Balanced Mind to restore balance to the Thinking Mind. (In the next chapter, we will use the Balanced Mind to restore balance to the Feeling Mind.) There is one key concept you will learn in this chapter that will help your Balanced Mind restore balance to the Thinking Mind: *dialectical thinking*.

Some people are just more rigid or "black and white" in how they think. People who have been traumatized are especially prone to thinking in extremes. Why is that? Because trauma survivors really have been in extreme situations. When we are in a life-or-death situation, there really aren't too many shades of gray worth contemplating! Unfortunately, sometimes those extreme ways of thinking crystallize into how we see everything else in life—even situations that are not traumatic.

Based on our previous life experiences, we learn to see things in a certain way, and only in that way. Even if we learn that what we *feel* is sometimes misleading, we often still assume that what we *think* must be gospel truth. However, the reality is that not everything we think is necessarily completely true, accurate, logical, rational, or healthy. Once again, this can especially be true if we have been traumatized in any way. For instance, trauma survivors may inappropriately blame themselves for their own abuse. Or they may become overly negative in how they view themselves, other people who are not abusive, or even all of life.

You might remember from the first chapter that dialectics is all about finding balance by bringing together opposites. Dialectical thinking, also known as *balanced thinking*, simply means that we learn to bring our extreme thoughts and beliefs more to the middle. Balanced thinking means we learn to think about things from new and different perspectives—instead of thinking about things in only one way. Balanced thinking also means that we are flexible in how we think, that we can change our thinking if we learn new evidence, and that we can see things from someone else's perspective. People who learn to develop balanced thought patterns are better problem solvers, better at getting along with other people, and better at dealing with life in general.

Here is a preview of what you will learn in this chapter:

- How to connect your Thoughts, Emotions, and Actions (TEA)

- How to identify a variety of Automatic Negative Thoughts (ANTs)

- How to challenge your ANTs with three simple stomps

- How to center your thinking by working the TOM (Thought, Opposite, Middle)

WHAT'S IN YOUR TEA?

Psychologists have long noticed that thoughts, emotions, and actions all influence each other. Since the 1960s, psychologists have especially focused on how certain thoughts can trigger certain emotions, which in turn can instigate certain actions. More recent research, however, has shown that this relationship is not so simple or linear. Rather, emotions affect our thinking just as much as thoughts affect our emotions. In fact, our thinking affects both our emotions and our actions; our emotions affect both our actions and our thoughts; and our behaviors affect both our thoughts and our emotions (Shoda and LeeTiernan 2002, among others). So basically, everything affects everything else!

Since thoughts, emotions, and actions all influence each other, what that also means is that if you change one, you can also change the other two. Some aspects of this workbook focus directly on changing our behaviors (such as the previous chapter). Other aspects of this workbook focus directly on changing our emotions (such as the next chapter). However, this chapter focuses on changing our thinking, for two reasons. First, just because we think something does not mean that it is 100 percent accurate. Second, sometimes it becomes easier to change our emotional or behavioral reactions if we can also change how we think about something.

Although thoughts, emotions, and behaviors all mutually affect each other, in this lesson we are going to specifically focus on the sequence that has received the most attention and research:

thoughts $\longrightarrow$ emotions $\longrightarrow$ actions

In fact, this sequence is so well known that I have created the following acronym to help you remember it better: TEA. That's why in this lesson we are going to learn what's in your TEA.

Let's use a simple example to show how this sequence can sometimes play out. Let's assume you were verbally abused by your father growing up. Now let's assume that you are terrified every time your boss asks to speak to you, and therefore you try to avoid him at all costs. It seems that your boss is causing you all this distress, right? But is that really the case? Well, let's find out what's in your TEA. The reality is that you are probably having thoughts such as, *What does he want now? He's probably going to just criticize me.* And those thoughts probably cause you to feel scared of or intimidated by him. And those emotions probably lead you to avoid him whenever possible.

I want you to notice a few things from this example. First of all, this sequence makes complete sense based on your experiences growing up with a verbally abusive father. Your father really did criticize you.

You had good reason to feel scared of and intimidated by your father. And you also had good reason to avoid him as much as possible. But does this sequence necessarily apply to your boss? Maybe it does and maybe it doesn't!

The second thing I want you to notice from this sequence is that it might be your thoughts about your boss—and not necessarily your boss himself—that are driving this sequence. Since you are thinking that he is going to criticize you (like your father used to do), then of course you are going to feel intimated, and of course you will want to avoid him.

The final thing I want you to notice about this sequence is that it is *self-reinforcing*. What does that mean? It simply means that the more the sequence plays out, the more it will continue to play out. The more you think your boss will criticize you, the more you will feel intimated by him. The more you feel intimated by him, the more you will avoid him. And the more you avoid him, the more you will fear his criticism. And the cycle just keeps going! This cycle is sometimes called a *self-fulfilling prophecy*.

So what would happen if you simply changed how you thought about your boss? Instead of constantly dreading potential criticism, what if your thoughts were the following: *My boss has always praised me much more than criticized me. Sometimes he gets a little short and irritable, but that's only when he's under lots of stress himself. So when he gets that way, it's probably more about him than me.* If that's what you were thinking, how would that change your emotions? You might still feel a little scared or a little intimated, but would it be as intense as before? And would you still feel such a strong need to avoid him at all costs? Do you see how simply shifting your perspective can also make it a little bit easier to change your emotions and actions as well?

Let's take a closer look at some of these concepts.

Let's Have a TEA Party!

Review the differences between thoughts and feelings (refer back to chapter 1). Write down three examples of thoughts and three examples of their related feelings below.

Thoughts	Feelings
I can't stand my boss.	Anger

Situations themselves are rarely the only reason for our emotional or behavioral reactions. Rather, it's how we *think* about the situation that often influences how we *feel* about the situation, which in turn influences our actions. Briefly describe a recent situation, then try to map out the connection between thoughts, feelings, and behaviors.

Situation: _____

My Thought About the Situation	→	My Emotion	→	My Action
I said "hi" and she didn't even respond—what a snob!	→	Anger	→	Avoid her in the future.
	→		→	
	→		→	
	→		→	

Now take the same exact situation and look at it from your Balanced Mind. Map out how a different interpretation of the same situation could have resulted in a different emotion and different behavior.

Different Thought	→	Different Emotion	→	Different Action
Usually she says "hi" back—maybe she's preoccupied with something.	→	Compassion	→	Check in later to see if she's okay.
	→		→	
	→		→	
	→		→	

If our thoughts are misguided, then our emotions will be misguided, and then our actions will also be misguided. I call this the domino effect. Provide one example of this sequence; start by briefly describing the situation.

Situation: _____

Unhealthy Thought	→	Unhealthy Emotion	→	Unhealthy Action
I am such a failure at life.	→	Self-hate	→	Self-harm
	→		→	
	→		→	
	→		→	

Have you ever tried to stop an emotion in the middle of the emotion? Or stop an action in the middle of the action? That's pretty hard, right? That's because the more this sequence gets going, the harder it is to stop. I call this the train effect. What are three emotions and three behaviors that are really hard for you to stop when you are right in the middle of experiencing them?

Difficult Emotions to Stop	Difficult Actions to Stop
1.	1.
2.	2.
3.	3.

Have you ever had a self-fulfilling prophecy? Did your thoughts about a situation ever make the situation come true? Or make the situation even worse? Let's look at this example, then fill out the chart on your own.

Situation: My wife looks like she is frustrated about something.		
Thoughts: I bet she's frustrated with me. I can never make her happy.	Emotions: My own frustration.	Actions: Become defensive and ask her: "Now what's your problem?"
Even worse situation: Wife gets even more frustrated, or becomes frustrated if she wasn't already.		

Your turn!

Situation:		
Thoughts:	Emotions:	Actions:
Even worse situation:		

What's in My TEA?

Describe three situations demonstrating the relationship between thoughts, emotions, and actions.

Situation 1: _____

_____

_____

_____

_____

This is what I thought about the situation: _____

_____

_____

_____

These were my emotions: _____

_____

_____

_____

These were my actions: _____

_____

_____

_____

Situation 2: _____

_____

_____

_____

_____

This is what I thought about the situation: _____

_____

_____

_____

These were my emotions: _____

_____

_____

_____

These were my actions: _____

_____

_____

_____

Situation 3: _____

_____

_____

_____

This is what I thought about the situation: _____

_____

_____

_____

These were my emotions: _____

_____

_____

_____

These were my actions: _____

_____

_____

_____

So far in this chapter, we have learned that thoughts, emotions, and actions all influence each other. In these exercises, we have decided to focus on one specific sequence: the way in which our thoughts about something influence how we feel about it, which in turn influences how we react. As we have learned, however, not everything we think is completely logical, accurate, or rational. Especially if we have been traumatized, we tend to have extreme thought patterns, which in turn can set us up for extreme reactions. Therefore, one way to balance our emotions and actions is to first balance our thinking. But before we learn how to do that, we first need to recognize examples of unbalanced thought patterns.

STOMPING THE ANTS

Have you ever looked at yourself in one of those funny mirrors? Whose image did you see? It was you, of course…but it wasn't *exactly* you. You were either taller or shorter or fatter or skinnier (or all of the above) than you are in real life. In other words, the image you were seeing was indeed you—but a *distorted* version of you.

That's what distorted thoughts are like. Distortions happen when whatever we think about a situation is somehow skewed—it's kind of accurate but not *completely* accurate. Or maybe these thoughts used to be accurate for a past situation but are no longer fully accurate for the current situation. Usually these distortions are completely automatic and tend to be overly negative—and that's precisely why I call them *automatic negative thoughts*, or ANTs for short.

Psychologists have long noticed that we tend to have what is called a *negativity bias* (Siegel 2014). One example of the negativity bias is that our brain tends to favor false alarms over no alarms. Think of our ancestors in the jungle. Let's assume one ancestor sees a stick but thinks it's a snake. That ancestor will experience anxiety—but survive. Now let's assume another ancestor sees a snake but thinks it's a stick. That ancestor will not experience anxiety—and will probably die! Do you see how the negativity bias helps us survive, but at the cost of anxiety?

Another example of the negativity bias is that our brain learns from negative experiences much more quickly than it learns from positive experiences. If you don't believe me, just think about this: How many insults does it take to wipe out many compliments? Only one! And how many compliments does it take to undo one insult? Many!

The negativity bias explains why trauma is so traumatizing: Because of how we are hardwired, really negative experiences (a.k.a. trauma) stick in our mind for a really long time. It can be extremely difficult to unlearn what has been learned from traumatic experiences.

Traumatized people have the same negativity bias as everyone else, just more of it. As we have already learned, trauma is an extreme situation that throws us, and our thoughts, off balance. Trauma survivors tend to have more extreme thinking in several ways: what I call the *three P's* and the *hindsight bias*. The three P's are *personal, permanent,* and *pervasive*. This means when something bad happens to you, you take it more personally than other people, you think it's more permanent than it really is, and you also think it is more pervasive than it really is. The hindsight bias means that you beat yourself up over everything that could've or should've been done differently to stop the bad thing from happening.

Trauma, by definition, really is personal, pervasive, and permanent. For example, let's assume you were raped after a work party. The rape was personal: It happened to you. The rape was pervasive: It affected every aspect of your life. Maybe you could not concentrate at work; maybe your relationship with your husband suffered; maybe you were more irritable with your kids. And the rape was permanent: It could not be undone. Furthermore, you may never see males again in the same way. In addition, you would probably have all kinds of thoughts about what you could or should have done differently to prevent the rape you didn't know would happen (the hindsight bias).

In short, trauma directly triggers the three P's plus the hindsight bias. But the real problem happens when we start to use that thinking with everything else in life: *Everything is personal, everything is pervasive, everything is permanent, and everything could have been prevented.* The three P's and the hindsight bias are examples of automatic negative thoughts. Here are some more ANTs that you might recognize (adapted from Beck 2011):

- **All or Nothing:** when you think everything is either black or white, and you do not take into account possible shades of gray. Absolute terms (such as "always" and "never") are sure signs of this sort of thinking.

  Example: "I am never thin enough. I am always so obese."

- **Overgeneralizing:** when you take one small piece of evidence and apply it across the board. Overgeneralizing is a great example of making something more permanent or more pervasive than it really is.

  Example: "All men are potential predators."

- **Mental Filter:** when you fixate on only one negative event, or whenever everything seems dark and negative (sort of like wearing a dark pair of sunglasses).

  Example: "Life has been awful ever since the accident. Life will never ever be the same again."

- **Disqualifying the Positives:** when you explain away or discount something that is legitimately positive.

  Example: "The new girl said I was really nice, but it's only because she doesn't know my history yet."

- **Mind Reading:** when you believe that you know what someone else is thinking or feeling. This type of thinking tends to result in self-fulfilling prophecies.

  Example: "She didn't even wave to me today; I bet she's mad at me about something. Fine, if that's how she's going to be, then I will just ignore her too!"

- **Fortune-Telling:** when you think for sure that you know how an event in the future will turn out. This type of thinking also tends to result in self-fulfilling prophecies.

  Example: "There's no way that I am going to pass my biology test tomorrow, so why even bother studying for it?"

- **Magnifying:** when you take a small problem and turn it into a large problem.

  Example: "I can't believe I didn't make the basketball team. This is *so* humiliating. Everyone is going to think that I am such a loser!"

- **Catastrophizing:** when you take a small problem and turn it into an outright crisis. This type of thinking is "magnification on steroids."

  Example: "I can't believe I didn't make the basketball team. I am seriously thinking about killing myself."

- **Minimizing:** when you take a large problem and turn it into a small problem. This type of thinking is the opposite of magnification.

  Example: "He hit me, but it doesn't really hurt. I can cover up the bruise with makeup and no one will know."

- **Denial:** when you take a large problem and turn it into no problem at all. This thought process is "minimization on steroids." This is also the opposite of catastrophizing.

  Example: "A little bit of physical contact in marriage is not domestic violence. Physical contact shows that we love and care about each other!"

- **Emotional Reasoning:** when you think with your feelings; in other words, feelings become facts. Or put another way, emotions become the only evidence you need.

  Example: "I feel really guilty about the miscarriage; I know that it wouldn't have happened if I never got pregnant in the first place!"

- **Over-Shoulding:** when you pile up unreasonable or unrealistic expectations for yourself. One example of over-shoulding is the hindsight bias, which we discussed earlier.

  Example: "I should have known better than to wear that outfit to the party. Of course I got raped."

- **Under-Shoulding:** when you do not take ownership for things that really are your responsibility.

  Example: "They shouldn't get all upset when I pop positive on my drug screen, because they don't know what kind of a life I've had."

- **Labeling:** when you complete the following sentence in unfavorable terms: "I am _____." Even labels we consider to be accurate are still distortions, since they only focus on one sliver of information while ignoring other relevant data points.

  Example: "I am such a loser; I deserve the poor treatment I get."

- **Personalizing:** when you take something personally that has nothing to do with you. Blaming yourself for someone else's abuse is the harshest form of personalizing.

  Example: "The only reason he molested me is because I was such a slut."

- **Blame Shifting:** when you blame someone else for something that really is your responsibility. This type of thinking is often the opposite of personalizing.

  Example: "I wouldn't have punched him if he wasn't screaming at me first."

- **Rationalizing:** when you try to make something seem logically right, even though it was wrong.

  Example: "Technically he didn't mean to rape me. He just loved me so much that he couldn't control himself."

- **Justifying:** when you try to make something seem morally right, even though it was wrong.

  Example: "He didn't mean to rape me. It was my duty as his girlfriend to make sure he was satisfied."

All of these automatic negative thoughts are like swarms of ANTs that can cause lots of harm to yourself and others. Fortunately, there are three simple questions that can help you identify a potential ANT:

Is it logical?

Is there evidence?

Does it matter?

Each time you answer no to one of these questions represents one stomp on an ANT. And remember, you only have to stomp an ANT one time to kill it!

My Pet ANTs

Do you have any pet ANTs? Refer to the long list of automatic negative thoughts and identify the five types of ANTs that you use the most. Then provide a personal example of each one.

ANTs	Example

Stomping on My ANTs

Now let's practice stomping those ANTs! Identify a recent situation in which your thinking may have been inaccurate. Next, identify which ANT needs to be stomped. Then ask yourself the three ANT-stomping questions. An example is provided.

What was the situation?

Today is our anniversary and my husband has not even said anything yet!

What was I thinking about the situation?

I bet he forgot. Or worse, he probably forgot on purpose. Maybe he doesn't even love me anymore. Is he having an affair?

Which type of ANT was I using?

- Personalizing—I might be taking something personally that might have nothing to do with me.

- Mind Reading—I might be assuming I know what's going on in his mind.

- Emotional Reasoning—I might be "thinking" with my feelings; in other words, I might be using my own emotions as the evidence.

Question 1: Is it logical? If no, why not?

Yes, it's logical that he could have forgotten the anniversary. After all, one year he really did forget.

Question 2: Is there evidence? If no, why not?

There is absolutely no evidence that he is having an affair.

Question 3: Does it matter? If no, why not?

Well, of course our anniversary matters!

Based on your responses to these three questions, what is your final conclusion about this situation?

One year he really did completely forget our anniversary. But last year, he pretended to forget...but then came home with the best surprise ever. I wonder what's up his sleeve this year?

Now it's your turn to try this exercise.

What was the situation? _____

_____

_____

_____

_____

What was I thinking about the situation? _____

_____

_____

_____

_____

Which type of ANT was I using? _____

_____

_____

_____

_____

Question 1: Is it logical? If no, why not? _____

_____

_____

_____

_____

Question 2: Is there evidence? If no, why not? _____

_____

_____

_____

_____

Question 3: Does it matter? If no, why not? _____

_____

_____

_____

_____

Based on your responses to these three questions, what is your final conclusion about this situation?

_____

_____

_____

_____

In this lesson, we learned a variety of thought patterns that tend to characterize unbalanced thinking. I call these various thinking errors automatic negative thoughts, or ANTs for short. We also learned three simple questions to help identify a potential ANT: Is it logical? Is there evidence? Does it matter? As we learned, we only have to answer "no" to one of these questions in order to stomp an ANT!

WORKING THE TOM

In this lesson, we are going to learn a simple way to transform those unhealthy thoughts (our ANTs) into healthier ones. I call this skill *Working the TOM*. You can execute this skill in three simple steps: Thought, Opposite, Middle.

Step 1. Thought: First, identify one of those pesky ANTs that you learned in the previous lesson. Let's assume your thought is: *All guys are predators and only want one thing.*

Step 2. Opposite: Now let's identify the exact opposite of that thought: *All males in human history are completely innocent and would never do anything to exploit another human being.*

Step 3. Middle: Now let's identify a thought somewhere in the middle: *Some people are predators but most people are not. The key is to learn which people to trust and which people to avoid.*

Which of these three thoughts is the most accurate? Which thought is the healthiest way to live your life? Even though the first thought may have once seemed accurate based on your own life experiences, is it still the most accurate? Do you see how the first thought will exclude you from healthy relationships with people who really are safe? Do you also see how the opposite thought is naive and will only set you up for further victimization? Finally, do you see how the middle thought is the best approach to dealing with life and people? Many people call this middle thought the Balanced Response or the Middle Path.

This process is called *dialectical thinking*, or *balanced thinking*, which is the entire purpose of this chapter. As you learned at the beginning of this chapter, balanced thinking means learning to think in the middle instead of at the extremes. It means learning to see things from new and different perspectives instead of thinking about things in only one way. Finally, balanced thinking also means that we are flexible in how we think, that we can change our thinking if we learn new evidence, and that we can see things from someone else's perspective.

Besides working the TOM, here are some more tips for balanced thinking:

- Avoid words such as "always" and "never."

- Practice looking at other points of view.

- Remember that no one has the absolute truth (except God).

- Use "I feel" statements.

- Remind yourself that the only constant is change.

- Accept that different opinions can be equally valid.

- Consider that we all have both good and bad qualities.

- Check out your assumptions.

- Do not put words in other people's mouths.

- Do not expect others to read your mind.

- Think about how everyone is different and what a gift that is.

Working the TOM

Now let's practice the three-step process with TOM. First we will identify a particular thought; then we will identify the exact opposite of that thought; and then we will identify a more balanced thought in the middle. Later on in this exercise, you will see how quickly and drastically you can downregulate your emotions just by shifting your thoughts more to the middle.

1. Do you remember any of your automatic negative thoughts, or ANTs, from the previous lesson? Identify one of your ANTs here. Since this is just practice, it does not have to be the worst one. Example: "I feel so overweight. I look disgusting."

Thought: _____

_____

2. Now identify the opposite extreme of that thought. Make the opposite as silly, exaggerated, irrational, or comical as possible. Example: "The Barbie doll was designed from my personal replica. I am clearly Miss Universe. In fact, if there were another universe, I would be Miss Universe there too."

Opposite: _____

_____

3. Now identify a more balanced middle thought, somewhere in between the two extremes. Remember, there is no single correct middle thought. In fact, it is perfectly possible—and preferable!—to have multiple middle thoughts.

Example: "Maybe I am still a tad pleasantly plump, but I am also really proud of all of the weight I have lost so far!"

Middle: _____

_____

4. Of the three options (thought, opposite, middle), which of the three is the most accurate, logical, rational, or reasonable? Why?

_____

_____

_____

_____

_____

5. What emotions do you feel when you have the original thought? How much do you feel that emotion on a scale of 1 to 100? Example: "I feel depressed when I think about being overweight and how disgusting I look. I am at 75 percent for depressed."

Emotion for original thought: _____ **Intensity of emotion (1–100):** _____

6. Now, what emotions would you feel if you truly believed the middle thought? It's okay if you don't fully believe it yet. But for the sake of argument, how would you feel if you did believe the middle thought? Example: "I would still feel a little depressed that I haven't reached my goals yet, but I would also be encouraged by all the progress I've made. I would be at 25 percent for depressed."

Emotion for original thought: _____ **Intensity of emotion (1–100):** _____

Did you notice how quickly and dramatically emotions can change just by changing your original thought? And what's truly amazing about this little trick is that you did not even change anything in reality; rather, all you had to do was change how you think about reality!

Consider the following example to further illustrate this point: If you walked in the room and it was 75 degrees, and then five minutes later it was 25 degrees when you left, would you notice the difference in temperature? This is literally how much influence you can have over your emotional climate, just by changing your thoughts!

Of course, having the middle thought does not instantly or automatically cancel out the original thought. However, at the very least, the original thought now has some competition!

7. Now let's practice working the TOM. First, write down one negative Thought about yourself. Next, identify the exact Opposite of that belief. Then, identify a thought that lies somewhere in the Middle. Which thought do you think is logically the most accurate? Repeat this two more times.

Thought: _____

_____

Opposite: _____

_____

Middle: _____

_____

Which belief is logically the most accurate? _____

_____

Thought: _____

_____

Opposite: _____

_____

Middle: _____

_____

Which belief is logically the most accurate? _____

_____

Thought: _____

_____

Opposite: _____

_____

Middle: _____

_____

Which belief is logically the most accurate? _____

_____

So far in this chapter, we have learned that thoughts influence emotions, which influence actions. In addition, we learned some common examples of unbalanced thoughts. In these exercises, we practiced a simple three-step process for balancing our extreme thoughts: thought, opposite, middle. As you can see, TOM is one balanced dude! In the next lesson, we will continue to practice our balancing act.

THE BALANCING ACT

Up to this point, we have learned that unbalanced thinking can lead to unbalanced emotions and unbalanced actions. That's why we have learned to identify specific types of unbalanced thoughts and how to bring those extreme thoughts more to the middle. For some people, working the TOM (thought, opposite, middle) is all they need to think more flexibly. But for others, it can be helpful to go into more detail.

How to Improve Balanced Thinking

In this lesson, you will learn a methodical process for engaging your Balanced Mind that integrates all of the concepts you have learned so far. You can be on your way to more-balanced thinking in just ten steps!

1. Identify a problem situation.
2. Identify your thoughts regarding this situation.
3. Identify your emotions about this situation.
4. Identify your actions toward this situation.
5. Identify any automatic negative thoughts about this situation.
6. Identify the exact opposite of your ANTs.
7. Identify a middle thought that is in between your original thought and its opposite thought.
8. Identify your new emotions about this situation.
9. Identify your new actions toward this situation.

10. Ask yourself: *Is my new way of dealing with the situation more effective than the original one?*

Let's get started! The following exercise will guide you through each step.

Ten Steps to Improve Balanced Thinking

Think of a recent situation that you wish had not happened. Now identify your specific thoughts, emotions, and actions regarding the situation.

1. **Situation:** _____

_____

_____

_____

2. **Thoughts:** _____

_____

_____

_____

3. **Emotions:** _____

_____

_____

_____

4. **Actions:** _____

_____

_____

_____

Remember those pesky ANTs we talked about earlier in this chapter? Did you notice any ANTs in your thoughts about this particular situation? If so, what were they? Are your thinking errors making a bad situation even worse? Are your thinking errors causing even more issues than the situation itself?

5. Any ANTs?

ANT 1: _____

_____

_____

_____

ANT 2: _____

_____

_____

_____

ANT 3: _____

_____

_____

_____

Now identify the opposite thought of your original thought, followed by the middle thought.

6. Opposite thought: _____

_____

_____

_____

7. Middle thought: _____

_____

_____

_____

Finally, let's assume you truly believe the middle thought. What are your new feelings and actions? Did they change?

8. New emotions: _____

_____

_____

_____

9. New actions: _____

_____

_____

_____

Remember that it is sometimes possible to generate new emotions and new actions simply by changing our thinking. More often than not, our new TEA will help us deal with the problem situation more effectively than our old TEA—even if we can't change anything about the situation itself! In the final analysis, ask yourself:

10. Is my new way of dealing with the situation more effective than the original way? Explain your response:

_____

_____

_____

_____

_____

_____

Congratulations! You've now worked through all ten steps. Even though it may have been challenging, the process will get easier with practice. Complete this exercise as many times as you need to get the hang of these skills. In this lesson, we learned how to use our Balanced Mind to change our thinking. First, we threw another TEA party by exploring our thoughts, emotions, and actions. Next, we practiced looking for ANTs in the TEA (automatic negative thoughts). And finally, we saw how TOM deals with these ANTs (thought, opposite, middle).

THE LAST WORD

In this chapter, we learned how to balance our thinking. Balanced thinking simply means bringing our extreme thoughts and beliefs more to the middle. Balanced thinking means thinking about things from new and different perspectives instead of in only one way. Balanced thinking also means being flexible in how we think, being able to change our thinking if we learn new evidence, and having the ability to see things from someone else's perspective.

In particular, we learned a series of acronyms to help us think more flexibly. First, we learned to examine what's in our TEA. In other words, we learned to identify our thoughts, feelings, and actions toward any particular situation. As you may recall, it becomes easier to deal with extreme emotions or extreme reactions when we first balance our extreme thinking. Next, we learned to identify ANTs, which are sometimes lurking in our TEA. Remember that ANTs represent automatic negative thoughts? ANTs will definitely ruin your TEA! Then we learned a simple three-step method for getting rid of ANTs by working the TOM (thoughts, opposite, middle). One way to remember all three acronyms is the following sentence: TOM does not like ANTs in his TEA.

Now that you have learned to balance the Thinking Mind, in the next chapter you will learn to balance your Feeling Mind. Get ready for some more acronyms, because you're about to "sow some SEEDS."

CHAPTER 5

Restoring Balance with Emotions

In the previous chapter, we learned how to use the Balanced Mind to bring balance to our Thinking Mind. In this chapter, we will learn how to use the Balanced Mind to bring balance to our Feeling Mind.

Do you sometimes feel like your emotions control you…more than you control them? It is normal for people who have been traumatized to experience intense emotions that seem to come out of nowhere. In fact, trauma survivors tend to experience five distinct patterns with their emotions.

First, you may have more negative emotions than others (such as more depression, more anxiety, or more anger). Second, your emotions might be more easily triggered. Third, your emotions may also tend to be more intense. Fourth, your emotions may take longer to return to their normal state. When you put all these patterns together, it's no wonder that your emotions can seem so unpredictable and overwhelming. And that's precisely why trauma survivors also experience a fifth trend: doing anything it takes to numb out as many of these overwhelming emotions as possible!

But now do you see how we are back to the problem of extremes? What would we ever do without the Balanced Mind? The good news is that DBT helps us balance our emotions by teaching us how to *manage* them. Now notice that I did not write "control"—I wrote "manage." Our emotions do not need to be controlled. In fact, trying to control our emotions will only make them feel even more unheard, unappreciated, and unrecognized—and then they will just have to scream even louder to get our attention!

Pretend each of your emotions is a different kind of vegetable. As we discussed in chapter 2, you wouldn't try to control, coerce, or manipulate vegetables, would you? But if you want this beautiful vegetable garden to flourish, you will certainly have to manage the garden. For example, you will need to plant the right seeds, check the soil, protect against predators, and remember to weed and fertilize.

In this chapter, you will learn six different strategies for managing your garden of emotions:

- Sow your SEEDS

- Weed the myths

- Check the soil

- Act the opposite

- Troubleshoot

- Fertilize with ABCs

Each of these strategies will help nurture your garden. But first, let's get started with planting!

SOW YOUR SEEDS

One of the best ways to nurture your emotions (believe it or not) is to take care of your body. Think of the last time you were sick. Or the last time you missed a meal. Or the last time you ate way too much. Or the last time you were hung over. Or the last time you didn't sleep the whole night. Were you a happy camper? Were you at the top of your game? Or is it fair to say you were more cranky, more depressed, or less "with it"?

Well, here are five simple "SEEDS" for taking care of your body—and, therefore, your emotions:

S—Symptoms

E—Eating

E—Exercise

D—Drugs

S—Sleep

Seed 1: Take Care of Your Symptoms

It is normal for trauma survivors to have more medical problems than other people. In fact, one famous study found that the more traumatic experiences we have as children, the more medical problems we are likely to have as adults (Curran 2016). If you are sick or your body is injured, make sure you take care of the symptoms! Each time your body has a symptom, it is actually crying out for help. So learn to pay attention to what your body is trying to tell you.

One leading trauma expert (Van der Kolk 2014) said that all healing from trauma starts with this step. Consult with a medical professional if you feel you need additional help with your physical symptoms.

Seed 2: Eat Well

It is normal for trauma survivors to experience problems with appetite and diet (Berk-Clark et al. 2018). Sometimes they eat too much and sometimes they don't eat enough. Remember the problem of extremes? Make sure you are consuming a balanced diet of healthy foods. This doesn't mean you have to become a health nut; it simply means you need to include healthy foods (such as fruits and vegetables) in your daily diet.

And it also means learning to balance your portions: not too much and not too little. How can your emotions be balanced if your diet isn't even balanced? Remember what grandma used to say? You are what you eat! Consult with a dietician or nutritionist if you feel you need additional help with your diet.

Seed 3: Exercise Daily

It is normal for trauma survivors to avoid any physical activity or sensations that remind them of their traumatic experiences (Van der Kolk 2014). Unfortunately, exercise tends to fall in that category, since exercise can cause the body to feel certain aches and pains that you would rather forget. This is tragic, since it is well known that just a little bit of exercise releases chemicals in our brain that improve our mood.

But let's be realistic: Exercise doesn't mean you need to start training for the Olympic trials. It simply means that you need to engage in some kind of physical activity on a daily basis. My personal philosophy of exercise is this: Don't make it so painful that you dread doing it again—and therefore make excuses not to! Instead, just do enough exercise to lift your mood. That will help you want to do it again. Remember the old saying, "Moderation in all things." Consult with a personal trainer if you feel you need additional help setting up an exercise routine.

Seed 4: Be Careful What Drugs Go into Your Body

Many trauma survivors use alcohol, street drugs, or other substances to "help" manage their painful emotions (Van der Kolk 2014). The problem is this: Although these chemicals may provide quick relief, as soon as the effects wear off, our emotions will feel even more out of control than before.

If your doctor prescribes certain medications to help regulate your emotions, that is fine. But if you want to balance your emotions, it is really important to take *only* the drugs—and dosages—that have been prescribed by your physician. Consult with a doctor or therapist if you feel you need medications to help balance your emotions.

Seed 5: Get Enough Sleep

Trauma survivors also tend to have a tough time sleeping at night (American Psychiatric Association 2013). Sometimes they have nightmares. Sometimes their minds just won't shut off. Sometimes they worry all night. And sometimes they even worry about not getting enough sleep!

Unfortunately, it is really hard to have balanced emotions during the day when you haven't slept well at night. Everyone has a different sleep schedule and rhythm, and some people need more sleep than others. But what everyone has in common is that we all need a good night's rest. How can you score A's in the game of life when you haven't even gotten your Z's? Consult with a doctor or therapist if you feel you need additional help with your sleep routine.

Sowing My SEEDS

Now it's your turn to dig into your garden, so to speak.

Seed 1: Symptoms

What physical symptoms did I experience this week? _____

_____

_____

_____

Do I need to see a doctor for any of these symptoms? _____

_____

_____

_____

What can I do to improve these symptoms? _____

_____

_____

_____

Seed 2: Eating

What did I eat this week? Did I have a balanced diet?

- Breakfast: _____

  _____

  _____

  _____

- Lunch: _____

  _____

  _____

  _____

- Supper: _____

_____

_____

_____

What can I do to improve my diet? _____

_____

_____

_____

Seed 3: Exercise

What did I do for exercise this week? _____

_____

_____

_____

Was it too much exercise, not enough exercise, or just right? _____

_____

_____

_____

What can I do to improve my exercise routine? _____

_____

_____

_____

Seed 4: Drugs

What substances did I consume this week? _____

_____

_____

_____

Were they prescribed? Did I follow the correct dosage? _____

_____

_____

_____

How can I better regulate which substances enter my body? _____

_____

_____

_____

Seed 5: Sleep

How many hours of sleep did I get this week? _____

_____

_____

_____

Did I follow a sleep schedule? _____

_____

_____

_____

What can I do to improve my sleep routine? _____

_____

_____

_____

Daily "Sow Your SEEDS" Chart

Did you sow your SEEDS for a healthy emotion garden? Place a check mark for each "seed" that you planted this week. Please include a brief summary of each seed. Below is a sample.

Symptoms	Eating	Exercise	Drugs	Sleep
✓ I had a migraine in the afternoon, so I did what my doctor told me to do.	I missed breakfast, I barely had time for lunch, and I splurged on junk for supper. Not a good diet day!	✓ I went for a 15-minute walk around the block.	✓ I took my prescribed antidepressant. I did not drink or consume street drugs.	I only slept for 5 hours. I wish I could have slept more, but the baby kept waking up, and I had to go into work early today.

	Symptoms	Eating	Exercise	Drugs	Sleep
Monday					
Tuesday					
Wednesday					
Thursday					

			Growth Areas:
Friday	Saturday	Sunday	

Tally all your check marks for the week. Then use this scorecard to get an idea of how well you're sowing your SEEDS.

31–35 ✓ = A+ Amazing! You rock! You are well on your way toward much better physical and emotional health.

26–30 ✓ = A Keep up the good work! With just a few more improvements, you will feel even better!

21–25 ✓ = B+ You're off to a great start! The more you practice self-care, the more these habits will become second nature.

16–20 ✓ = B That's great that you have some healthy habits! What will it take to boost these numbers even more?

11–15 ✓ = C+ Looks like you have some good days and some off days. What are you doing well on the good days that you could start applying to your off days?

6–10 ✓ = C Looks like you are currently prioritizing other things in your life more than your physical health. Do not hesitate to consult with a professional if you can't bring these numbers up on your own.

0–5 ✓ = D Consider asking a medical or counseling professional for tips on how to take better care of your body. You may need to receive treatment from a specialist (e.g., nutritionist, substance abuse counselor, etc.).

To cultivate a healthy garden of vegetables, we first need to plant the right seeds. The same concept applies to our emotions. Improving our emotions starts with learning how to take care of our bodies. In this lesson, we learned five different ways of doing just that. Now that we have planted the right SEEDS, we need to tend to our garden. In the next lesson, we will learn how to "weed out" the plants that do not belong.

WEED THE MYTHS

Myths are often used to explain why certain things are the way they are, and they tend to get told over and over again. Myths often combine some things that are true with other things that are not true.

Even if they are not completely true, myths are believed for the following three reasons: (1) We hear the same myth so often that eventually we start to believe that it must be true; (2) someone in authority teaches us the myth, so therefore we assume it must be correct; and (3) we agree with the explanation provided by the myth.

So here's the problem with myths: If we hear them enough, especially by someone in authority, and if we agree with their explanations, we tend to believe them—even if they are not true! Maybe you have heard an ancient myth (such as how the zebra got its stripes) that now seems funny, silly, and even entertaining to modern people. Why? Because we know the explanation provided by the myth is simply not true—no matter how many times we hear the story and no matter who tells it to us. Unfortunately, however, modern people still believe many myths for the three reasons mentioned above. And some of the greatest myths told in our times are about our emotions!

Trauma survivors in particular have often been taught many myths about their emotions. The messages we hear about our emotions often meet all the criteria for myths: They provide explanations, but fact is often mixed with fiction. And yet, we believe these myths anyway because (1) we hear these messages over and over; (2) the messages often come from our own parents, coaches, or spouses; and (3) we actually agree with their explanations.

Here's an example of an emotional myth. Let's assume someone in authority (such as your parent) has told you over and over again for many years that the reason you struggle with emotions is because you have a bad attitude. Since the messenger was your mother or father, and since you heard the message so often, you started to believe it. More important, at some point you believed this myth because you agreed with the explanation: "The reason my emotions are so overwhelming is because I have a bad attitude!"

This myth is simply not true. Perhaps you can remember many times when you had a good attitude, and your emotions were overwhelming anyway. But since you already believed the myth, you did not even notice the evidence that contradicted it. I call this concept our "emotional mythology." Unfortunately, believing myths about our emotions does not make them easier to manage. On the contrary, emotional myths can make our emotions even more overwhelming!

Here are some common myths that many people believe about emotions:

Myth 1:   Emotions are random and have no purpose.

Myth 2:   Becoming emotional means losing control.

Myth 3:   Emotions are either correct or incorrect.

Myth 4:   Only weak people talk about their emotions.

Myth 5:   Negative emotions are caused by a bad attitude.

Myth 6:   Painful emotions are dangerous and destructive.

Myth 7:   The only way to deal with negative emotions is to ignore them.

Myth 8:   Other people know what my emotions should be better than I do.

Myths can also be gender specific. Here are two more:

Myth 9:   Girls should not express anger; they should be nice!

Myth 10:   Boys should not cry; they should be tough!

Let's process a few of these myths together to learn what is untrue about each of these messages. And then let's identify some of your own emotional myths.

Myth 1: Emotions are random and have no purpose.

Weed the myth: Emotions are far from pointless. In fact, we could not survive as a species without them! Emotions such as fear help us to react quickly to immediate danger when we don't have the luxury to stop and think and form a plan. Emotions such as love and anger provide the motivation to accomplish great tasks, even at much personal cost.

Our emotions not only influence us, they also influence others. In fact, emotions are our greatest source of communication. Think of babies. Could babies survive without emotions? No! Babies learn to communicate through emotions long before they learn to communicate through words. Even with the amazing gift of fully developed language, which makes humans very unique among the animals, communication experts tell us that we still communicate more nonverbally than verbally (Frank 2016). And emotions allow us to do that.

What's a more accurate belief about emotions than this myth?

_____

_____

_____

_____

Myth 2: Becoming emotional means losing control.

Weed the myth: When we become emotional, sometimes we *feel* like we are losing control, especially if we are in the presence of other people, which makes us more self-conscious. But is it possible to be emotional and not lose control of our behaviors? Or is it possible to be nonemotional and still lose control of our behaviors? The answer to both questions is yes.

In fact, our jails are full of people who have been out of control, and very often the reason is because they do not have *enough* emotions! For example, people with antisocial personality disorder tend to have the most aggressive tendencies of all personality disorders (American Psychiatric Association 2013). And do you know why individuals with this disorder can be so aggressive? Is it because they have too many emotions? No! The reason their behaviors are sometimes so out of control is precisely because they *lack* such basic emotions as guilt, remorse, compassion, empathy, and other key emotions.

What's a more accurate belief about emotions than this myth?

_____

_____

_____

_____

Myth 3: Emotions are either correct or incorrect.

Weed the myth: Is there really only one right or one wrong way to feel in any given situation? At a wedding, is it possible for some people to be happy and some people to be sad? So then who is right and who is wrong? Is it possible for the same person to feel both sad and happy at the same time? If so, then is that person both right and wrong at the same time?

One leading expert reports that there are forty-three different facial muscles that outwardly express our inner emotions (Duenwalk 2005). What if we disagree with our emotions? Does that mean that all forty-three muscles are also wrong? Or does it simply mean the muscles are telling us how we feel?

What's a more accurate belief about emotions than this myth?

_____

_____

_____

_____

Now it's your turn to weed some myths. Describe how each of the following myths is inaccurate, and then write down some more accurate beliefs for each of them.

Myth 4: Only weak people talk about their emotions.

Weed the myth: _____

_____

_____

_____

More accurate belief: _____

_____

_____

_____

Myth 5: Negative emotions are caused by a bad attitude.

Weed the myth: _____

_____

_____

_____

More accurate belief: _____

_____

_____

_____

Myth 6: Painful emotions are dangerous and destructive.

Weed the myth: _____

_____

_____

_____

More accurate belief: _____

_____

_____

_____

Myth 7: The only way to deal with negative emotions is to ignore them.

Weed the myth: _____

_____

_____

_____

More accurate belief: _____

_____

_____

_____

Myth 8: Other people know what my emotions should be better than I do.

Weed the myth: _____

_____

_____

_____

More accurate belief: _____

_____

_____

_____

My Personal Myths

Are there any other myths you believe about emotions in general? What about myths you or others have about your own emotions? Write these down, along with what a more accurate belief would be.

Other myths I have believed about my emotions:	More accurate beliefs:

In this chapter, we have been learning how to nurture (not control) our garden of emotions. First, we learned how to plant the right SEEDS by taking care of our body. Next, we learned how to weed out our emotion myths by challenging them with more-accurate beliefs. But for this garden of emotions to flourish, we also need to make sure we have the right soil!

CHECK THE SOIL

Sometimes when we have really intense emotions, it's because we are reacting to either incomplete or inaccurate information. In other words, maybe some of the information is missing, or maybe some of the information is not completely correct. Once we have the right facts, however, it becomes easier to reset our emotions to match the actual situation. Just like a real vegetable garden needs the right soil, our emotion garden also needs the right facts.

Here are a few basic questions that can help us sort through just about any situation that seems to be triggering intense emotions. This is how we check the soil:

What are the facts of the situation?

What is true and what is not true?

What information am I missing?

What is the worst-case scenario?

How likely is the worst-case scenario on a scale of 1 to 100?

Will I die if the worst-case scenario happens?

How can I cope with the worst-case scenario?

What is the best-case scenario?

What is the most likely scenario?

How can I cope with the most likely scenario?

Let's try out an example before you practice this on your own. Let's assume your partner just came home late from work, for the second time this week. You are livid. Let's check the soil!

Checking the Soil

What are the facts of the situation?

My husband arrived 25 minutes late on Tuesday.

My husband arrived 35 minutes late on Thursday.

My husband did not call me either time to let me know.

My husband usually calls me when he knows he is going to be late.

What is true and what is not true?

True: This is not characteristic of my husband.

True: My husband has been complaining a lot about his boss and deadlines.

Not true: I have been noticing signs that my husband is cheating on me.

What information am I missing?

I don't fully know what's going on with his work situation right now. I need to have a conversation with him about his professional life.

What is the worst-case scenario?

My husband is having an affair with the boss he keeps complaining about.

How likely is the worst-case scenario on a scale of 1 to 100?

Anything is possible these days, but this one is pretty unlikely. Let's go with 5.

Will I die if the worst-case scenario happens?

No, I will not die. But my husband might! ☺

How can I cope with the worst-case scenario?

We would need to get into marriage counseling ASAP. Assuming I don't strangle him first!

What is the best-case scenario?

My dear husband not only works so hard for his family, but he is also always so considerate and thoughtful.

I am sure he spent all afternoon trying to text me, but his phone probably died from work overload.

What is the most likely scenario?

He is probably overwhelmed with work stuff. When this happens, he tends to become less considerate about letting me know what's going on in his work life.

How can I cope with the most likely scenario?

After he has time to unwind this evening, we need to have a little chat about communication.

Now it's your turn! Let's practice checking the soil.

What are the facts of the situation?

_____

_____

_____

_____

What is true and what is not true?

_____

_____

_____

_____

What information am I missing?

_____

_____

_____

_____

What is the worst-case scenario?

_____

_____

_____

_____

How likely is the worst-case scenario on a scale of 1 to 100?

_____

_____

_____

_____

Will I die if the worst-case scenario happens?

_____

_____

_____

_____

How can I cope with the worst-case scenario?

_____

_____

_____

_____

What is the best-case scenario?

_____

_____

_____

_____

What is the most likely scenario?

_____

_____

_____

_____

How can I cope with the most likely scenario?

_____

_____

_____

_____

So far in this chapter, we have been learning how to nurture our garden of emotions. We have learned how to plant the right SEEDS (by taking care of our body), how to weed out misconceptions (about emotions themselves), and how to make sure we have the right soil (by checking the facts).

But what if one day you just don't want to work on this stupid garden anymore? Even worse, what if you want to destroy the garden? What if you want to uproot the plants? Yank out the seeds? Poison the soil? When you are in this type of mood, one of the best things you can do to your garden of emotions is the exact opposite of what you feel like doing.

ACTING OPPOSITE

Have you ever noticed that reacting to some of your emotions can actually make them worse? For example, let's suppose that you are really ticked off. And when you get ticked off, you clench your fists and raise your voice. Have you noticed that the more you clench your fists and raise your voice, the angrier you get?

Now let's suppose you are feeling really sad, and you just want to sleep, isolate, and crawl into your bed and never come out. Have you noticed that the more you sleep and isolate, the sadder you feel?

Or let's suppose you are terrified of your boss, and you prefer to avoid her at all costs. Have you noticed that the more you avoid your boss, the more you become scared of her?

In each of these situations, there are actually two things going on: First there is an emotion, and then there is an urge. Some urges are healthy, because they help your emotions stabilize. For example, let's assume that every time you feel sad, your urge is to call your friend and sip gourmet coffee. This kind of response would probably help you feel better.

In other words, not all emotions are triggering, and not all urges are problematic. But sometimes we get caught in a vicious cycle in which certain emotions trigger certain urges, and those urges (if acted on) only make the original emotion more intense and therefore more difficult to manage. When that happens, we now have a *trigger emotion* and a *problem urge*. And since both make each other worse, we are now stuck in a trap!

I call this trap the *stupid cycle*. We all get stuck in the stupid cycle. Getting stuck in the stupid cycle doesn't mean, of course, that you are actually stupid. It simply means that you are probably not using your Balanced Mind whenever you get stuck in this trap!

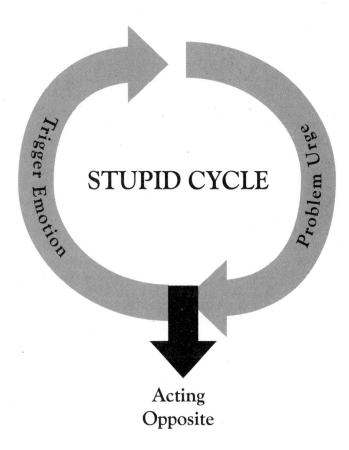

So how do we get out of the stupid cycle? So glad you asked! It's much easier—and harder—than you think. On one hand, it's a really simple concept: All you have to do to get out of the stupid cycle is the exact opposite of what you feel like doing. On the other hand, this is a really, really difficult concept to apply: No one wants to do the exact opposite of what they feel like doing! So even though *acting opposite* is a really easy concept to understand, learning to apply it is quite a different story—and requires *lots* of practice and willingness.

But before we start practicing this new skill, I want to make a few quick points about the term "trigger emotions." First of all, I chose this term over "negative emotions" because not all trigger emotions feel negative. In fact, some feel positive! For instance, have you ever made poor decisions when you fell in love with someone too quickly?

Another reason I did not use the term "negative emotions" is because, with some trigger emotions, you don't feel anything at all! For example, have you ever made poor decisions when you were feeling bored or numb? And a final reason I did not use the term "negative emotions" is because I did not want to imply the myth that some emotions are bad and therefore should be avoided. As we have learned earlier in this book, *all* emotions (even the ones we don't like) provide extremely valuable functions.

A final message I would like to communicate before we get started with some practice is this: Of course doing the opposite of what you really want to do will not feel natural. Of course you will feel "fake" when you are just beginning to practice this skill. And that's exactly why I call this skill "acting" opposite! It's okay if you feel as if you are just acting or faking it. This is what I tell my own clients: "Fake it till you make it!"

Now let's explore some common emotions and how to respond to them using the skill of acting opposite. Take the time to write down your responses, even if it feels a little fake at first.

Acting Opposite with Anger

When I feel angry, I feel like doing these problem urges:

_____

_____

_____

_____

_____

When I do these urges, this is how I make the situation worse:

_____

_____

_____

_____

_____

Here are the opposites of my problem urges:

_____

_____

_____

_____

_____

If I do the opposite of my problem urges, this is how the situation could turn out:

_____

_____

_____

_____

_____

Acting Opposite with Sadness

When I feel sad, I feel like doing these problem urges:

_____

_____

_____

_____

_____

When I do these urges, this is how I make the situation worse:

_____

_____

_____

_____

_____

Here are the opposites of my problem urges:

_____

_____

_____

_____

_____

If I do the opposite of my problem urges, this is how the situation could turn out:

_____

_____

_____

_____

_____

Acting Opposite with Another Emotion

When I feel _____, I feel like doing these problem urges:

_____

_____

_____

_____

_____

When I do these urges, this is how I make the situation worse:

_____

_____

_____

_____

_____

Here are the opposites of my problem urges:

_____

_____

_____

_____

_____

If I do the opposite of my problem urges, this is how the situation could turn out:

_____

_____

_____

_____

_____

Acting Opposite with One More Emotion

When I feel _____, I feel like doing these problem urges:

_____

_____

_____

_____

_____

When I do these urges, this is how I make the situation worse:

_____

_____

_____

_____

_____

Here are the opposites of my problem urges:

_____

_____

_____

_____

_____

If I do the opposite of my problem urges, this is how the situation could turn out:

_____

_____

_____

_____

_____

Acting Opposite Chart

Fill out this chart to come up with a game plan for what you can do when you are triggered by various emotions.

Trigger Emotion	Problem Urge	Opposite Action
When I feel:	*I feel like doing:*	*What I can do instead:*
Angry		
Sad		
Bored		
Scared		
Excited		
Other:		

Other:		
Other:		
Other:		
Other:		

Throughout this chapter, we have been learning how to nurture our garden of emotions. For example, we have learned how to plant the right SEEDS (by taking care of our body), how to weed out misconceptions (about emotions themselves), and how to make sure we have the right soil (by checking the facts). In this lesson, we learned how to do the exact opposite of our urges when they are destructive or make our emotions feel even more intense or overwhelming. Just like uprooting the vegetables or poisoning the soil would not help a real garden, acting on our destructive urges does not help our emotion garden either.

But sometimes, no matter how much we try to nurture this garden, the predators attack anyway. And sometimes the predators attack from all angles at once. You better take aim, because in the next lesson, we are going to learn how to troubleshoot—or, rather, shoot our troubles!

TROUBLESHOOTING

When it comes to the game of life, do you have trouble shooting? Or have you learned to shoot your troubles? Now, I am not a violent person, but please work with my analogy: If we are going to protect our garden of emotions, we may have to shoot some predators! And life is full of them: work, deadlines, appointments, bills, illness…you get the point.

Sometimes we feel overwhelmed because life really is overwhelming. This is especially true for trauma survivors. Sometimes our problems pile up higher than dirty laundry—and we don't even know where to start. Sometimes the best way to manage overwhelming emotions is to start troubleshooting our stressors—one bullet at a time.

Here are ten bullets to improve our aim. Now, instead of having trouble shooting, let's shoot our troubles (Godley and Smith 2016).

1. Define the problem.

2. Brainstorm possible solutions.

3. Eliminate unwanted solutions.

4. Select one possible solution.

5. Identify possible obstacles.

6. Address each obstacle with a plan.

7. Try out the solution you selected.

8. Evaluate the outcome.

9. If necessary, try another solution.

10. If you're really stuck, ask a trusted friend or counselor to help you through this process.

First, let's practice this together. Let's troubleshoot the following problem:

Alexander is supposed to graduate this year. The only problem: He is currently failing *all* of his subjects.

Notice that you have already completed step 1!

1. Define the problem.

Alexander is supposed to graduate this year. However, he is currently failing all of his subjects.

2. Brainstorm possible solutions.

- Yell, swear, and throw random objects.

- Complain to all of my friends.

- Ground him for the rest of the school year (it's currently October).

- Schedule a meeting with all of his teachers and coaches.

3. Eliminate unwanted solutions.

I always complain to all my friends. That never changes anything, but it does help me feel better. So that one stays. Yelling, swearing, and throwing random objects sounds tempting but will probably not earn me the respect I need to deal with this situation. At least not effectively. Grounding for the rest of the school year also sounds tempting, but (A) I don't actually want him around the house 24/7 for the next 7 months, and (B) he might just give up completely if he doesn't have a chance to redeem himself. After all, he is very motivated by sports! Scheduling a meeting with the teachers and coaches is probably the most effective step to take.

4. Select one possible solution.

I am going to select two solutions: Complain to all my friends and schedule a meeting with all the teachers and coaches.

5. Identify possible obstacles.

- I might have to take time off from work.

- My husband might have to take time off from work.

- It's a nightmare to get a meeting scheduled with just one teacher or coach, much less the whole lot of them at once!

6. Address each obstacle with a plan.

Just getting this meeting scheduled is going to require lots of coordination and flexibility. But I do know that the school faculty usually meets on Thursday mornings before school starts. If we can schedule a meeting then, we won't have to finagle a gazillion different schedules, and my husband and I probably won't even be that late to work.

7. Try out the solution you selected.

I reached out to the guidance counselor with my concerns and a suggestion for a Thursday meeting. She echoed my concerns and thought a Thursday meeting was a great idea, but we would have to meet before the faculty meeting. I said no problem!

8. Evaluate the outcome.

My husband had to work the first shift and wasn't able to take off for a non-emergency, so I went by myself. The meeting with the teachers and football coach went well. The teachers reported that the main reason Alexander's grades are low is because of missing assignments that he had started but had not turned in yet. They were all willing to offer partial credit for late assignments, which would bring his grades up to passing. The football coach agreed to bench Alexander until all assignments were in. This will be a huge motivator for Alexander, because he was supposed to start this season. Also, if Alexander fails the semester, he will not be eligible for track in the spring either. Another big motivator!

9. If necessary, try another solution.

Even though the meeting was much more of a success than I expected, I still want to complain to my friends!

10. If you're really stuck, ask a trusted friend or counselor to help you through this process.

If Alexander continues to fail his classes, I will reach out to the guidance counselor again. Maybe there are deeper issues here than just academics?

Now it's your turn to shoot some troubles!

1. Define the problem.

_____

_____

_____

_____

_____

2. Brainstorm possible solutions. Try to come up with at least four possible solutions.

_____

_____

_____

_____

_____

_____

3. Eliminate unwanted solutions. Cross out the solutions you can't see yourself doing. Explain why.

_____

_____

_____

_____

4. Select one potential solution. Explain why you chose it.

_____

_____

_____

_____

5. Identify possible obstacles.

_____

_____

_____

_____

_____

_____

6. Address each obstacle with a plan.

_____

_____

_____

_____

_____

_____

7. Try out the solution you selected. Make it your homework assignment for this week! Write down where and when you will try it.

_____

_____

_____

_____

8. Evaluate the outcome. Was your plan effective? Ineffective? Which obstacles got in the way?

_____

_____

_____

_____

_____

_____

9. If necessary, try another solution. The first solution may not have worked, and, if so, that's okay. Write down the solution you would like to try next.

_____

_____

_____

_____

10. If you're really stuck, ask a trusted friend or counselor to help you through this process. Make a list of people who can help you identify effective solutions—and implement them!

_____

_____

_____

_____

_____

_____

_____

Throughout this chapter, we have learned all about how to grow an emotion garden. We have learned how to plant the right SEEDS (by taking care of our body), how to weed out misconceptions (about emotions themselves), how to make sure we have the right soil (by checking the facts), and how to act opposite when we feel like nuking this garden off the map. In this lesson, we even learned how to shoot the predators with a ten-bullet process designed to troubleshoot our peskiest problems. But there's still one more thing this garden needs to thrive: fertilizer!

FERTILIZE WITH ABCS

Would you ever plant a garden in the spring and just abandon it until the end of the summer? Even if you planted the right seeds, what kind of outcome would you expect if you did absolutely nothing to maintain the garden? Well, the same concept applies to your emotions. Now that your garden of emotions has been planted, we need to fertilize it! In this final lesson of this chapter, you will learn the ABCs of maintaining emotional stability (Linehan 2015):

A—Add positives

B—Build mastery

C—Cope ahead

Do you recall the Coping Card you created in chapter 3? Remember that the whole point of that Coping Card was to give you tools for coping in a crisis? But what if you didn't wait for a crisis to use your coping skills? What if you used your coping skills…every single day? In other words, what if you switched from a reactive approach to life to a proactive approach? The whole point of this lesson is to make sure the various coping strategies you have learned throughout this workbook become part of your daily routine, your new lifestyle, and the new *you*!

Let's discuss each of these ABCs in a little more detail:

Add Positives

Adding positives means doing something that makes you feel happy—every single day! We all feel better when good things happen to us. But why wait for a good thing to just happen? Why not schedule it instead? This strategy can be as simple as blocking off time for sipping a hot cup of coffee or watching a sunset.

Not surprisingly, research shows that simply adding positive experiences to our daily routines helps improve our mood and coping ability (Hutchinson et al. 2003). This is a great investment, when you consider that adding positive experiences to your life does not have to cost money or take a lot of time.

Build Mastery

Building mastery means doing something that you are good at—every single day! We all feel better about ourselves when we are productive or do something constructive. This strategy can be as simple as strumming your guitar, playing sports, or learning a new language. Building mastery is all about identifying your talents and then making goals to develop these gifts. This, in turn, will help you feel more secure and more confident in your abilities.

Research shows that having a sense of purpose or accomplishment can also help improve our mood and coping ability (Matthieu, Lawrence, and Robertson-Blackmore 2017). One way to build mastery into your life is to set SMART goals for yourself (refer to chapter 1).

Cope Ahead

Coping ahead means planning ahead for difficult situations. People who have experienced chronic trauma tend to become reactive as opposed to proactive. However, instead of just waiting for the next situation to happen, why not think of all the skills you already know? Why not visualize using those skills? Why not think of the trusted people in your life who can help you with the situation? Why not practice and role-play the skills ahead of time?

In one study of 182 college women with trauma histories, researchers found that students who coped ahead had fewer PTSD symptoms, *regardless* of the severity of the trauma, extent of the previous trauma history, or the amount of time elapsed since the trauma occurred (Vernon, Dillon, and Steiner 2009).

Let's Learn Our ABCs!

As you can see, the key to maintaining your beautiful garden of emotions is to fertilize with ABCs—every single day! Let's apply each of these fertilizers to your own personal life.

A—Add Positives

What are three simple things I really enjoy?

1. _____

   _____

2. _____

   _____

3. _____

   _____

B—Build Mastery

What are three of my strengths, gifts, or talents?

1. _____

   _____

2. _____

   _____

3. _____

   _____

C—Cope Ahead

1. What is a difficult situation I might have to face?

   _____

   _____

   _____

2. What skills have I already learned to face this situation?

_____

_____

_____

_____

_____

_____

3. Who can I trust to help me prepare for this situation?

_____

_____

_____

_____

_____

_____

Based on my ABCs, here are three goals I would like to set for myself:

1. _____

_____

2. _____

_____

3. _____

_____

Throughout this chapter, we have learned the complete process of nurturing an emotion garden. We started by learning to plant the right SEEDS (by taking care of our body). Next we learned to weed out misconceptions (about emotions themselves) while making sure we have the right soil (by checking the facts). Then we learned to troubleshoot when problems in life threaten to level the garden, or to act opposite when we feel like nuking the garden ourselves. In the final lesson of this chapter, we learned the importance of fertilizing this garden—every single day—with the following three actions: adding positives, building mastery, and coping ahead.

THE LAST WORD

In this chapter, we learned how to use the Balanced Mind to balance our Feeling Mind. Trauma survivors tend to have intense, unpredictable emotions. That's why they often try to either control or numb these emotions. Unfortunately, these approaches make emotions even more unbalanced and more difficult to manage. That's why we used a garden analogy throughout this chapter: If you want a healthy garden, it wouldn't make much sense to control or ignore the vegetables. However, it makes a whole lot more sense to plant the right seeds, weed the myths, check the soil, act opposite, shoot the troubles, and fertilize every day with ABCs!

CHAPTER 6

Restoring Balance with Relationships

At the beginning of this workbook, we learned that trauma has a way of throwing us off balance. Just about everything can get thrown off balance by trauma: our thoughts, our feelings, and our actions.

The same applies to our relationships. In fact, research shows that trauma caused by people induces much more emotional damage than trauma caused by natural disasters, such as hurricanes and tornadoes (Fowler at al. 2013). That's because as people we need people. And when people hurt us…it really, really hurts. Therefore, when trauma involves people, all of our relationships are potentially affected: personal relationships, professional relationships, intimate relationships, and even spiritual relationships. Not only are our relationships knocked off balance, they are also forced to the extremes—just like everything else. When we have been traumatized, we often learn to become either too passive or too aggressive—or both!

So far in this workbook, you have learned lots of skills to find balance with your thoughts, feelings, and behaviors. Now it's time to start finding balance in your relationships as well. In order to improve your relationships with other people, it's really important that you are using and practicing the skills you have learned so far.

Think about it this way: How can you be aware and accepting of other people if you are not even aware and accepting of yourself? How can you deal with other people's triggers if you cannot even deal with your own triggers? How can you respond to other people's thoughts and feelings if you cannot even regulate your own thoughts and feelings? Trust me, you will need all of these skills when it comes to relationships!

In this chapter, you will learn the middle path between reacting too passively versus reacting too aggressively. In particular, you will learn a simple formula (DEAR Adult) that will help you *assert* your perspective, *appreciate* someone else's perspective, and *apologize* when you have caused hurt or harm. In addition, you will learn how to do all of this with the right delivery, by using the Adult Voice (as opposed to the Child Voice or Parent Voice). By the end of this chapter, you will also learn how to nurture relationships that are worth nurturing, as well as untangle yourself from dysfunctional relationships that either need to change…or end.

RELATIONSHIP STYLES

Before we learn specific strategies on how to improve our relationship skills, it will be helpful to learn about four different relationship styles: passive, aggressive, passive-aggressive, and assertive.

Passive, Aggressive, and Passive-Aggressive

Remember fight, flight, and freeze from chapter 3? When it is not possible to escape a traumatic situation (flight), our only other options are either to remain passive (freeze) or to react with aggression (fight). With abuse in particular, either remaining passive or reacting aggressively can both be adaptive responses to stop the abuse from becoming even worse. And that is precisely why people who have been abused learn (or overlearn) to become either too passive or too aggressive with other things. But neither approach is a great strategy for the rest of life!

To be *passive* means that you do not speak up when other people take advantage of you. Passive means you are operating from a lose/win perspective: You let someone else get their way, while your wants and needs get sacrificed.

The opposite of passive is *aggressive*. To be aggressive means that you take advantage of someone else. Sometimes aggression can even include physical or verbal belligerence. Being aggressive means you are operating from a win/lose perspective: You get your way, even at the expense of someone else's wants or needs.

Not surprisingly, people who have been traumatized eventually learn that neither too much passivity nor too much aggressiveness is a great way to go through life. Too much passivity is no fun because other people just walk all over you. And too much aggressiveness either gets you in trouble or alienates other people. So that's when some people learn to become passive-aggressive!

As the term suggests, *passive-aggressive* is a compromise of sorts between these two extremes. To be passive-aggressive means that you get back at someone (which leans toward aggression), but you do it in a way that is indirect (which leans toward passivity). An example of passive-aggressive behavior might be spreading rumors about someone. On one hand, you are not acting completely passively, which would mean doing nothing at all. On the other hand, you are also not cussing out the person or stabbing them with pencils, which would be aggression. Rather, you are somewhere in the middle of the spectrum ranging from passive to aggressive.

Sometimes it might be appropriate to be passive, because not all battles are worth fighting; for example, if someone cuts you off in traffic, it might not do much good to retaliate with road rage. And sometimes it might be appropriate to be aggressive; for example, I for one would become quite aggressive if I ever witnessed a child being abused. And sometimes it might even be appropriate to be a little passive-aggressive; for example, if you are really frustrated with someone else's incompetence, it might be better to just mutter under your breath than to shout at full volume exactly what's on your mind.

Unfortunately, some people learn to overuse at least one of these tendencies. They tend to be too passive, too aggressive, or too passive-aggressive. And even though all three approaches are different, they have one thing in common: They are ineffective when overused. How so? The answer is less complicated than you might think: All three approaches require at least one loser! And no relational strategy will be effective in the long run if the relationship requires up front that at least one of the parties will not get their needs met.

Assertive

So now what? What's the missing link here? Is there *any* effective relational strategy? Is there any way to have a positive compromise between being too passive versus being too aggressive? Indeed there is. It's called being *assertive*! Assertiveness is a positive compromise between passive and aggressive for this simple reason: Assertiveness operates from a win/win perspective. Assertiveness means that my wants and needs are important—*and* so are yours!

In the rest of this chapter you will learn specific strategies for implementing assertiveness. The main tool you will be learning is DEAR Adult. This tool will teach you how to respectfully assert your perspective, how to appreciate someone else's perspective, and how to apologize when you cause hurt or harm.

Before we move on to learning the next skill, let's do some personal reflection. It will be really difficult to effectively move toward assertiveness and relational balance without first being able to recognize your default relationship style. So let's get started! Answer each question by providing at least one example.

Have I ever been passive with someone in a way that was unhealthy?

_____

_____

_____

_____

_____

Have I ever been passive in a healthy way?

_____

_____

_____

_____

_____

Have I ever been aggressive with someone in a way that was unhealthy?

_____

_____

_____

_____

_____

Have I ever been aggressive in a healthy way?

_____

_____

_____

_____

_____

Have I ever been passive-aggressive with someone in a way that was unhealthy?

_____

_____

_____

_____

_____

Have I ever been passive-aggressive in a healthy way?

_____

_____

_____

_____

_____

HOW TO ASSERT WITH DEAR ADULT

Regardless of how you are wired as a person, and regardless of how someone else is wired as a person, there are three A's that are indispensable for human interactions:

- **Assert**—Respectfully express your own needs and perspective

- **Appreciate**—Value the needs and perspective of other people

- **Apologize**—Offer to repair any damage you have caused in a relationship

You can think of these skills as the three legs of what I call the *relationship stool* (more on this later). If you can get these three skills down, you are well on your way to more effective communication—not to mention healthier relationships!

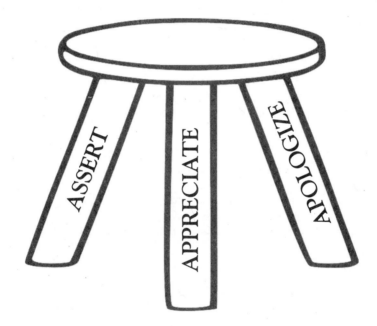

Now we are going to learn a simple formula that will help you develop each of the three skills. The formula is called *DEAR Adult*:

D—Define

E—Express

A—Assert

R—Reinforce

In this lesson, we will learn how to use DEAR Adult to assert (adapted from Linehan 2015). Let's start with a hypothetical scenario. Let's assume your roommate keeps leaving his dirty dishes in the sink, and you are the one who ends up washing them. You could ignore the problem and hope he finally gets the hint. Or you could go off the deep end and cuss him out. Either way, the problem might not get resolved. So let's learn a more effective way of dealing with this situation.

D—Describe

The first step is to simply *describe* the situation. However, when we describe, we need to stay as neutral, objective, and nonjudgmental as possible: just the facts. Do not blame, point fingers, or make assumptions. When you describe, it is also helpful to avoid dropping the "you" bomb whenever possible. As soon as you interject the word "you," the other person is likely to become defensive and might even counterattack. Therefore, it is helpful to frame the situation in terms of "I statements" and "we statements" instead of "you statements." This is a really good way to avoid the impression of blaming or pointing fingers.

Ineffective: "You never wash the stinking dishes, you little freak!!"

Effective: "I have noticed that we do not have a system in place to make sure the dishes get washed."

E—Express

Now that you have described the situation, you have established the necessary context to *express* how you feel about the situation. Once again, it is really important to avoid the "you" bomb whenever possible and to use "I statements" and "we statements" instead. It is fine at this point to mention any emotions that you might be feeling. However, be careful not to exaggerate your feelings either.

Ineffective: "You really tick me off whenever you are too lazy to wash your own stinking dishes!"

Effective: "It is frustrating that there are no clean cups when we want to get a drink of water. I feel like there's got to be a better system."

A—Assert

Now that you have described the situation, as well as expressed how you feel about the situation, you are in a much better position to finally *assert* yourself. To assert means that you ask people to change what they are doing. You may either ask people to stop doing something, to start doing something, or to alter what they are doing. Most people do not like to change. That is precisely why it is so important to first describe and first express before you attempt to assert. If you just assert out of the blue, with no context, people do not understand where you are coming from. But when you first describe the situation (nonjudgmentally), you provide the first layer of context. And then when you express how you feel about the situation (nonjudgmentally), you provide another layer of context. Now the other person not only understands that there is a problem, they also understand how you feel about the problem. In other words, your request will now make much more sense.

Ineffective: "So please get off your lazy butt and start washing the stinking dishes!"

Effective: "So I propose we set up a rotation. What if we take turns washing the dishes?"

R—Reinforce

This last step is crucial. Now that you have described, expressed, and asserted, it's really important to *reinforce* everything you have stated so far. Actually, there are two main things you want to reinforce: your *request* and the *relationship*. There are many ways of reinforcing both your request and the relationship. In my opinion, the best way of all is to explain that what you're asking for is a win/win proposition. In other words, explain how what you are requesting is actually in the best interest of the other person too. If you do not reinforce in this way, then everything you have been describing, expressing, and asserting so far might come across as "me, me, me." And as we all know, that's not the best way to convince anyone of anything. Therefore, it's really important to flip the "m" into a "w" and turn that "me" into a "we"!

Ineffective: "So have I been clear, or do you still not get it?"

Effective: "How about this: I will wash the dishes on Monday, Wednesday, Thursday, and Saturday, and you wash the dishes the other three days. I don't mind taking an extra day. And since it's Monday, I don't mind starting my rotation today. What do you think?"

Adult Voice

So far we have learned an important sequence: describe, express, assert, reinforce. While each of these steps is really important, so is something else: Your *delivery*. No matter how perfectly you articulate these steps, they will not work if you do not execute them the right way. In short, we need to deliver these steps like an adult—not like a child or parent.

Communication experts distinguish among three voices that we tend to use with other people (Berne 2015). Sometimes we use Parent Voice. That's when we yell, scream, condemn, criticize, lecture, scold, or berate someone else. I know this description kind of gives parents a bad rap, but think of the voice your parents used on you when they were really upset or lost it. And sometimes we use Child Voice. That's when we whine, pout, sulk, complain, or throw a temper tantrum. Think of the voice your kids use when they want something forbidden at the supermarket.

And sometimes we even use Adult Voice. This is the voice two adults use with each other when both are calm and collected. Now, I probably don't have to tell you which voice is the most effective: We all know that Adult Voice is the voice of reason. However, when we are triggered enough, we all default to either Parent Voice or Child Voice—even though they don't work!

Here are some qualities you need to know about Adult Voice:

- **Adult Voice is mindful.** In other words, Adult Voice is both aware and accepting!

- **Adult Voice is aware.** During a conversation, Adult Voice is aware of our words, volume, body language, facial expressions, triggers, timing, and proximity to the other person.

- **Adult Voice is accepting of all parties involved.** During a conversation, Adult Voice accepts the other person's wants and needs just as much as your wants and needs.

- **Adult Voice knows how to use distress tolerance skills.** When triggers arise in the conversation, Adult Voice puts coping skills to good use. What distress tolerance skills would help you in a difficult conversation?

- **Adult Voice knows how to use emotion regulation skills.** Adult Voice can manage difficult emotions that arise in the conversation, because it employs emotion regulation skills. Which of these coping skills would help you in a difficult conversation?

- **Adult Voice knows how to use dialectical thinking skills.** In other words, Adult Voice can avoid rigid or extreme thought patterns by knowing how to think flexibly and process information from someone else's perspective.

- **Adult Voice knows how to find the middle ground.** Adult Voice avoids power struggles and instead strives to find a win/win consensus through negotiation and compromise.

- **Adult Voice knows how to appear confident (not cocky!).** Adult Voice can recognize and avoid passive, aggressive, and passive-aggressive relational styles.

- **Adult Voice uses *connect talk* rather than *control talk*.** We tend to use control talk when we just "know" that we are right, and we just "know" the other person is wrong. Typical forms of control talk include commands, accusations, and blame. You know you are using control talk when you tell other people how they should think, feel, and act. The main problem with control talk is that it does not work! Control talk simply provokes the other person to become defensive, retaliate, escalate, or shut down. Think of the last time you felt controlled by someone. Did that make you want to comply with their expectations—or resist even more? Ultimately, control talk undermines rather than reinforces the relationship.

  Connect talk, on the other hand, means using inclusive words such as "we" and "us"—as opposed to making "me" versus "you" distinctions in the first place. Connect talk values the relationship more than being right or winning the blame game. Research shows that connect words are much better at persuading people than control words (Kehoe 2014).

- **Adult Voice knows how to take personal responsibility.** Adult Voice also knows how to offer to be part of the solution, instead of just blaming the other person or demanding that the other person change.

DEAR Adult—Assert

Before having a difficult conversation with someone, it is usually helpful to outline your thoughts first. Once you have your outline, you may even want to role-play your conversation with a friend or therapist. Ready to map out what you will say? Let's begin!

First, think of a difficult situation that needs to be confronted or corrected. Then, write down what you will say.

D—Describe the situation nonjudgmentally.

_____

_____

_____

_____

_____

_____

_____

_____

E—Express myself tactfully.

_____

_____

_____

_____

_____

_____

_____

_____

A—Assert my request diplomatically.

_____

_____

_____

_____

_____

_____

_____

_____

_____

R—Reinforce both my request and my relationship.

_____

_____

_____

_____

_____

_____

_____

_____

_____

Adult—Make a list of all the strategies (including DBT skills) I will need in order to stay grounded in my Adult Voice.

_____

_____

_____

_____

_____

_____

_____

_____

_____

_____

When you execute DEAR Adult in person, it's really important to stick to the script. When you are describing, just describe; do not jump ahead. When you are expressing, just express; do not jump ahead. And so forth.

Sticking to the script also means that you do not react to the other person's reactions. If you describe or express or assert, and the other person goes off on a tangent, just let them; do not follow their rabbit trail. Instead, just listen politely, and when they run out of steam—and eventually they will—simply move on to the next step of DEAR Adult.

The more you stay grounded by sticking to the script, the less you will reinforce the other person's tangents. This leaves the other person with two main options: either become more grounded like you, or start to look like an idiot. Either way, you have the home court advantage.

If you do not feel that you have the skills yet to pull off the DEAR Adult orally, you can do so in a letter. Use your outline as the foundation for a DEAR Adult letter. The "describe" part makes for a really good introductory paragraph; the "express" and "assert" parts make for really good middle paragraphs; and the "reinforce" part makes for a really good concluding paragraph. After you hand the person your letter, you can offer to discuss it in real time.

Now that we have learned to use the DEAR Adult formula to assert, let's use the same formula to implement two more functions of effective communication: appreciate and apologize.

HOW TO APPRECIATE AND APOLOGIZE WITH DEAR ADULT

No matter how well we assert, relationships will not work if that's all we do. Healthy relationships involve much more than just walking around and asserting yourself all day. On the contrary, balanced relationships require lots of give and take, lots of trial and error, and lots of repair work when they do not go like we expect them to. Just as we have needs that we want other people to meet, not surprisingly, other people also have needs that they want us to meet. And just like other people do not always meet our expectations, we do not always meet the expectations of other people either.

In short, if we only learn to assert well, our *relationship stool* only has one of the three necessary legs. The other two legs required for effective relationships are appreciation and apologies. The more you can appreciate the perspectives of other people and apologize when you have caused hurt or harm in a relationship, the more other people will be willing to meet your wants and needs as well. In other words, we need all three legs of the stool!

The good news is that we have already learned the DEAR Adult formula to assert. Now we can use the same formula to both appreciate and apologize. Here's how. Let's start off using DEAR Adult to appreciate someone else's perspective.

Appreciate

Here's a handy table illustrating the steps to using DEAR Adult to hone the skill of appreciation.

D—Describe	Summarize or paraphrase the main points of what the other person has stated.
E—Empathize	Instead of expressing your own feelings, empathize with the other person's emotions. Explain that you understand why they feel however they feel.
A—Appreciate	The word *appreciate* has three distinct but related meanings. Sometimes it simply means to understand. For example, if you tell your boss that you feel like you are working too many hours and she says, "I can appreciate that," what that means is that she gets what you are saying. More common is its meaning to value something or someone. For example, if your supervisor tells you, "I really appreciate you as an employer," that means that she values you. Appreciate also has a third meaning: to increase in value. For example, if you say, "The value of my house has appreciated," what you mean is that the value of your house has just increased. All three definitions apply to effective communication. If you want other people to respect your perspective, then you will also need to appreciate theirs: • Understand their perspective • Value their perspective • Add value to their perspective

R—Reinforce	Reinforce means either to strengthen something or to increase a behavior. When it comes to this formula, what we most want to reinforce is the ability of both parties to compromise and negotiate. After you have described the other person's perspective, empathized with the other person's perspective, and then even appreciated the other person's perspective, both of you are now in a much better position to find and reach a consensus.
Adult	Recall the ten qualities of Adult Voice. Remember to stay calm and centered by avoiding both the Parent Voice and the Child Voice.

Now it's time to use Dear Adult to practice being appreciative. Use the space below to outline your thoughts. Once you have your outline, you can practice with a friend or therapist. Then you can try the conversation face to face.

DEAR Adult—Appreciate

Think of a recent instance in which someone else expressed their opinion or made a request to you. Instead of immediately responding with your own opinion or request, why not first take some time to appreciate the other person's perspective?

D—Describe the other person's perspective by summarizing or paraphrasing.

_____

_____

_____

_____

_____

_____

_____

_____

_____

E—Empathize with the other person's emotions.

_____

_____

_____

_____

_____

_____

_____

_____

A—Appreciate the other person's perspective by understanding, valuing, and even adding value to their perspective.

_____

_____

_____

_____

_____

_____

_____

_____

R—Reinforce my appreciation (and our relationship) by fostering compromise, consensus, and win/win thinking.

_____

_____

_____

_____

_____

_____

_____

_____

_____

_____

Adult—Make a list of all the strategies (including DBT skills) I will need to stay grounded in my Adult Voice.

_____

_____

_____

_____

_____

_____

_____

_____

_____

_____

It would be great if everything in life could be resolved by either asserting our perspective or appreciating someone else's. Of course, that is not realistic. We all make mistakes, and sometimes we even cause hurt and harm to someone else. But fear not: DEAR Adult is once again coming to the rescue!

Apologize

Here's another table showing the steps to using DEAR Adult—this time to practice the skill of apologizing.

D—Describe	Describe what you did wrong.
E—Empathize	Empathize with the other person's perspective. Explain how your actions have affected the other person.
A—Apologize	State that you are sorry, that you regret what you did, and that you regret how your actions have affected the other person.
R—Reinforce	Of course, it's not enough to just say you are sorry, with no evidence that you are truly sorry. Remember that to reinforce means either to strengthen something or to increase a behavior. In this case, you need to strengthen your apology with some sort of follow-up, which in turn may increase the other person's willingness to forgive you. There are several ways to reinforce an apology, and all of them begin with R: *repair, restore, reconcile*. As we all know, words are cheap and actions speak louder than words—so the key to reinforcing an apology is to put your words into action. Explain what you will do differently in the future. Explain exactly how you will repair the damage, restore the situation, and reconcile the relationship. And then do it!
Adult	Recall the ten qualities of Adult Voice. Remember to stay calm and centered by avoiding both the Parent Voice and the Child Voice.

Now it's time to use Dear Adult to practice being apologetic. Use the space below to outline your thoughts. Once you have your outline, you can practice with a friend or therapist. Then you can have the conversation face to face.

DEAR Adult—Apologize

Think of someone you hurt. Recall what happened. Then, write down what you will say to sincerely express your apology.

D—Describe what I did wrong.

_____

_____

_____

_____

_____

_____

_____

_____

E—Empathize with the other person's emotions.

_____

_____

_____

_____

_____

_____

_____

_____

_____

_____

A—Apologize for what I did wrong.

_____

_____

_____

_____

_____

_____

_____

_____

_____

R—Reinforce my apology (and our relationship) by explaining how I will repair, restore, and reconcile.

_____

_____

_____

_____

_____

_____

_____

_____

_____

_____

Adult—Make a list of all the strategies (including DBT skills) I will need to stay grounded in my Adult Voice.

_____

_____

_____

_____

_____

_____

_____

_____

_____

_____

_____

Whether you are asserting, appreciating, or apologizing, you cannot forget to use Adult Voice. Remember that it does not matter how well you articulate these skills; if you do not use the correct voice, it will not work! In the next lesson, you will learn a simple tool that will help you balance—and bolster—your relationships even further.

LEARNING THE LOVE LANGUAGES

In the 1990s, a psychologist named Gary Chapman (2015) studied married couples. After years of research, Dr. Chapman noticed that people tend to both express and perceive affection in very predictable patterns. For example, some people feel more appreciated if we spend time with them or do a favor for them, while other people feel more appreciated if we give them something or say encouraging words, such as a compliment or praise. In addition, some people feel more appreciated with some sort of physical touch, such as a hug or tap on the shoulder. Dr. Chapman called these different ways to communicate affection the "five love languages":

- Gifts

- Time

- Touch

- Words

- Service

Dr. Chapman found that most people tend to have one or two preferred love languages. While our love languages may evolve over time or we may feel appreciated in several different ways at once, most of us feel the most appreciated in special ways.

Dr. Chapman also noticed that problems can occur in relationships when two people do not share the same love languages. For example, let's assume a father tries to shower affection on his teenage son by doing things for him, such as a changing the oil in his car. However, the son feels controlled whenever his father does things like this. Meanwhile, the father wonders why the son doesn't do more around the house. The son in turn tries really hard to do well in school and in sports, hoping for some modicum of praise from his father. However, instead of complimenting his son on his achievements, the father just complains that the son works hard everywhere except at his own house.

Do you see what's going on here? The father and son have different love languages! The father communicates affection through acts of service, while the son needs praise in order to feel appreciated. As a consequence of mismatched love languages, both the father and the son feel unappreciated—even though both are trying hard to express their appreciation!

As you can see, figuring out your own love language—not to mention the love language of others—can do wonders to help just about anyone improve their relationships. But this tool is especially important for people who have experienced trauma. Let me explain why. At the beginning of this chapter, I made the following statement: *Research shows that trauma caused by people inflicts much more long-term damage than trauma caused by natural disasters. That's because as people we need people. And when people hurt us…it really, really hurts.* Well, just like it is possible to demonstrate appreciation for people in terms of their love language, it is also possible to *hurt* people in terms of their love languages.

Let's assume that five-year-old Jacki's love language is touch. For example, Jacki loves to have her hair combed, loves to be hugged, and loves to be tucked into bed at night. The only problem is this: No one does this for her. Not surprisingly, Jacki does not feel loved. But to make matters worse, Jacki's mother physically abuses her whenever she gets drunk, while Jacki's father touches her inappropriately whenever *he* gets drunk. Of course, it goes without saying that both physical and sexual abuse are already damaging enough. But can you imagine how harmful these forms of abuse would be to someone whose love language is *touch*?

Now let's assume that Jacki's babysitter, Uncle Jim, has really taken a liking to Jacki. And Jacki *loves* the attention. Uncle Jim strokes her hair, rubs her back, and even tucks her into bed at night with goodnight kisses. As time goes on, however, Uncle Jim also starts to touch Jacki inappropriately.

Of all the forms of abuse mentioned so far, this one will probably cause Jacki the most long-term harm. Why? It will be easy for Jacki to learn that her mother and her father were both abusive, because she hated the forms of touch she received from them. But it can be quite difficult to process the acts of someone who meets your love language needs…and then hurts you in terms of that very same love language The confusion that results from this unresolvable contradiction causes untold psychological damage in children. And yet, this is exactly how predators are able to "groom" their victims for ongoing abuse.

So as you can see, there is a dark side to this concept of love languages. While love languages can explain how humans can meet each other's needs, they also explain one of the most devastating ways that people can also take advantage of other people. Our love languages not only give us the capacity to feel cherished and appreciated, they also set us up for exploitation. Of course, no one likes to get hurt in any form, but when we are harmed in terms of our love language, it hurts even more.

So how do we use the concept of love languages to improve the quality of our current relationships? Let's go back to the mindfulness formula we learned at the beginning of this book:

applied mindfulness = awareness + acceptance + action

First, we need to become more aware of our love languages (ours and others'). In addition, we need to become more aware of when love languages are either mutual or mismatched. We also need to become more aware of how our love languages make us vulnerable to exploitation, and how we have been hurt in terms of love languages. Finally, we also need to become more aware of how we express our love languages to others.

Some people excessively lavish a certain love language on other people as an attempt to get others to respond in kind. For example, have you ever met someone who constantly hugs other people, or is constantly complimenting everyone, or is constantly doing things for other people? The reason they constantly hug other people is because they are the ones who want the hug. The reason they constantly compliment someone else is because they are the ones who want a compliment back. However, there is a problem with this approach: Going over the top with your love language sometimes has the opposite effect of actually *pushing away* other people, because the other person feels controlled, manipulated, or smothered.

What's My Love Language?

It's really difficult to understand ourselves and our relationships with others if we don't understand our love languages. Answer the following questions to figure out the different ways you feel appreciated...or exploited. Has anyone ever tried to hurt you in terms of your love language?

Praise

Do I ever feel appreciated when people give me compliments? On a scale of 1 to 10, how appreciated do I feel when I receive a compliment? (10 = highest appreciation, 1 = lowest appreciation)

_____

What specifically do I like, want, or wish people would say to me?

_____

_____

_____

_____

_____

_____

Has anyone ever hurt me by the words they used? What did they say?

_____

_____

_____

_____

_____

_____

Did anyone ever give me compliments to get me to do harmful things? How so?

_____

_____

_____

_____

_____

_____

Gifts

Do I ever feel appreciated when people give me things? On a scale of 1 to 10, how appreciated do I feel when I receive a gift? (10 = highest appreciation, 1 = lowest appreciation)

_____

What specifically do I like, want, or wish people would give to me?

_____

_____

_____

_____

_____

_____

Did anyone ever give me things that were harmful? What were they?

_____

_____

_____

_____

_____

_____

Did anyone ever use gifts to get me to do harmful things? What were they?

_____

_____

_____

_____

_____

_____

Time

Do I ever feel appreciated when people spend time with me? On a scale of 1 to 10, how appreciated do I feel when someone spends time with me? (10 = highest appreciation, 1 = lowest appreciation)

_____

What specifically do I like, want, or wish people would do with me?

_____

_____

_____

_____

_____

_____

Did anyone ever spend time with me in ways that were harmful? How so?

_____

Did anyone ever spend time with me to get me to do harmful things? How so?

_____

_____

_____

_____

_____

_____

Service

Do I ever feel appreciated when people do favors for me? On a scale of 1 to 10, how appreciated do I feel when someone does something for me? (10 = highest appreciation, 1 = lowest appreciation)

_____

What specifically do I like, want, or wish people would do for me?

_____

_____

_____

_____

_____

_____

Did anyone ever do any "favors" for me that were actually harmful? How so?

_____

_____

_____

_____

_____

_____

Did anyone ever do favors for me to get me to do harmful things? How so?

_____

_____

_____

_____

_____

_____

Touch

Do I ever feel appreciated when people notice me through touch (such as hugs)? On a scale of 1 to 10, how appreciated do I feel when someone hugs me or pats me on the back? (10 = highest appreciation, 1 = lowest appreciation)

_____

How specifically do I like, want, or wish people would provide me with physical touch?

_____

_____

_____

_____

_____

_____

Did anyone ever provide me with physical touch in ways that were harmful? How so?

_____

_____

_____

_____

_____

_____

_____

Did anyone ever provide physical touch to get me to do harmful things? How so?

_____

_____

_____

_____

_____

_____

Reflect back on your responses. For which love language or languages did you score the highest? Which love languages have other people exploited? How can you apply this information to increase your mindfulness of current or future relationships?

_____

_____

_____

_____

_____

_____

_____

_____

Once we have become more aware of our love languages, we need to accept them. Maybe you don't like your love language. Maybe you wish you had a different one. Maybe you feel needy for wanting to feel loved in the first place. Maybe you feel like this whole "love language" spiel is a load of malarkey or only for wimps. Or maybe you find someone else's love language to be annoying or too high maintenance. Regardless of which glitches you face, the reality is that love is one of the greatest needs we have as humans, and relationships do not work very well if both parties involved cannot learn to mutually communicate appreciation. In short, love languages aren't going away anytime soon just because you do not like them!

Let's answer some more awareness and acceptance questions:

What are the love languages of the people closest to me? Write down their names and some examples.

_____

_____

_____

_____

_____

_____

_____

_____

What are some specific things I can do to express appreciation in terms of *their* love languages?

_____

_____

_____

_____

_____

_____

_____

_____

_____

Once we have increased both awareness and acceptance, it's now time to take action. Intentionally explain to other people how you feel appreciated. Intentionally ask other people how they feel appreciated. (In other words, do not try to read other people's minds, and do not expect them to read yours.) And then intentionally interact with other people in terms of *their* love languages—not yours! However, you will also need to intentionally distance yourself from people who seem to be exploiting your love language.

Moreover, you will also need to intentionally communicate affection to yourself, so that you are not always dependent on other people to meet all of your needs. For example, if you crave verbal encouragement, learn to provide yourself with positive affirmations. If you feel appreciated by gifts, spoil yourself once in a while with a special purchase. If you need physical touch, treat yourself to a massage. In short, show yourself some love! It's okay, really. In fact, here in DBT land, we even have a term for that: self-care.

What are some ways I can show self-appreciation by meeting my own love language needs?

_____

_____

_____

_____

_____

_____

_____

ENDING THE DRAMA CYCLE

So far in this chapter, we have learned a lot of information about how to improve relationships.

But what happens when we try all of this…and a relationship still does not work? What if we learn to be assertive, but the other person is aggressive? What if we learn to appreciate someone else's perspective, but the other person only criticizes? What if we apologize, but the other person only condemns? What if we use Adult Voice, but the other person only responds with Parent Voice? What if we think win/win, but the other person can only think win/lose? What if we try to meet someone else's love language, but that person only takes advantage of us?

This is certainly a possibility. Here's the reality: The best we can do in any relationship is use our own skills. Since our behaviors really do affect other people (in both positive and negative directions), using our skills really will go a long way to improve a lot of our relationships. People will notice that you are handling situations differently and, in most cases, that will prompt them to handle situations differently as well. Unfortunately, you can never force someone else to use the skills that you have been learning. No matter how hard you try, some people are simply unwilling or unable to change. Even worse: No matter how skilled you become in relationships, some people remain abusive.

Therefore, this final lesson on relational effectiveness is about learning to exit a dysfunctional, unhealthy, or abusive relationship that cannot be turned around, no matter how hard you try or how many skills you use. Let's face it: Finding balance in relationships is not just about improving the good ones; sometimes it's also about ending the bad ones.

In order to do this, we need to resort back to the same old message I've been harping on since the beginning of this book: awareness, acceptance, action. First, you need to become *aware* of the signs of a dysfunctional relationship. Second, you need to *accept* those signs (as opposed to ignoring, rationalizing, justifying, minimizing, or sugarcoating them). And third, you need to take *action*. In this case, action means keep using your DBT skills. But if a relationship remains unhealthy, then taking action might also mean exiting that relationship.

Let's start off with increasing our awareness by learning some telltale signs of dysfunctional relationships. Unhealthy relationships tend to involve three roles: *persecutor, victim,* and *rescuer* (Weinhold and Weinhold 2014). The persecutor is the person acting abusively; the victim is the person receiving the abuse; and the rescuer is the person attempting to save the victim from the persecutor. There are two ways these roles can play out. On one hand, sometimes there really is a persecutor, there really is a victim, and there really is a rescuer. On the other hand, sometimes these roles are just that: roles that people take on based on perceptions, miscommunication, and misunderstandings.

Let's start off discussing the second scenario first. Consider the following dysfunctional family: Let's assume a disgruntled father feels like he pulls all the weight at home and gets no respect. In short, he feels like a victim. So one day, the father decides to lay down the law by making his lazy kids do two hours of chores before school. Now the kids, who see dad as an unpredictable tyrant, also feel like the victims. But do the kids see dad as a victim? Of course not; they see dad as the persecutor! Then mom sees what's going on, so she decides to intervene on behalf of the children. Therefore, mom is now the rescuer. However, dad now feels even more like the victim, since his wife just undermined his paternal authority. But does dad see mom as the rescuer? No, he sees her as the persecutor! But, of course, the wife doesn't feel like the persecutor at all. On the contrary, she also feels like the victim—after all, she is simply trying to stand up for her kids! So now the kids see what is going on between the parents, and they decide to stick up for mom. So now who are the new rescuers? The new victims? The new persecutors? Do you see how this is going nowhere fast? Tragically, dysfunctional relational cycles like this one carry on for years and sometimes even decades.

Although this scenario is dysfunctional, it might also be redeemable. At some point, everyone in this family feels like the victim; at some point everyone thinks that someone else is the persecutor. And at some point, everyone takes on a rescuing role: Dad tries to rescue himself, mom tries to rescue the kids, and the kids try to rescue their mom. So much unnecessary drama happens whenever these three roles are present.

So what's the solution? You have already learned it! Everything you have learned in this chapter is the solution to this scenario. What if dad simply used a DEAR Adult to assert his perspective? What if mom used another DEAR Adult to assert her perspective? What if both parents used another DEAR Adult to both appreciate and apologize, as necessary? What if both parents remained mindful of each other's love languages? What if the husband realized that his wife simply needed some verbal encouragement while the wife realized her husband feels appreciated by acts of service? In short, what if both parents respectfully heard each other out, utilized win/win thinking, and collaboratively decided to create a new chore chart for their children, while soliciting input from the kids themselves? Do you see how simply using DBT skills causes all of these roles to evaporate? The persecutor stops acting like a persecutor, the victim stops acting like a victim, and the rescuer stops acting like a rescuer...and then the drama simply stops.

Once you are aware of and accept the signs of a dysfunctional relationship, sometimes the best course of action is to simply use your skills. Obviously, this approach is the most effective of all when everyone in the relationship is able and willing to use their skills. Sometimes the best way to exit a dysfunctional relationship is to be the necessary agent of change to transform the relationship into something healthier. You will know you are back in a healthy relationship when there is balance, acceptance, respect, and win/win thinking—and everyone's needs are being met.

However, all bets are off when there really is a persecutor, there really is a victim, and there really is a rescuer. If a husband batters his wife or a father molests his daughter, we do not use DBT skills—we call the cops and involve the authorities! In other words, these sorts of relationships need to be cut off immediately. If you know that a minor is being abused, then you need to be the rescuer. And if you are being abused as an adult, then you need to be your own rescuer. You simply cannot afford to wait for someone else to play that role!

Exiting the Drama Cycle

Now let's explore the roles you and your loved ones may play.

Have I ever taken on a dysfunctional persecutor role? What did that look like? How could I have exited that role?

_____

_____

_____

_____

_____

_____

_____

_____

_____

Have I ever taken on a dysfunctional victim role? What did that look like? How could I have exited that role?

_____

_____

_____

_____

_____

_____

_____

_____

_____

_____

Have I ever taken on a dysfunctional rescuer role? What did that look like? How could I have exited that role?

_____

_____

_____

_____

_____

_____

_____

_____

_____

What do I think is the difference between a healthy versus unhealthy rescuer role?

_____

_____

_____

_____

_____

_____

_____

_____

_____

Am I currently involved in any dysfunctional roles? If so, which ones? Can I use any of my DBT skills to transform this relationship from an unhealthy relationship into a healthy one? If so, which skills? If not, what is my exit plan for this relationship?

_____

_____

_____

_____

_____

_____

_____

_____

THE LAST WORD

Trauma disrupts balance in all aspects of our lives, including relationships. Trauma often causes us to take on extreme positions relative to other people. For example, we learn to become either too passive or too aggressive. In short, we need to find a middle path that helps us restore balance. In this chapter, we learned how to do that through four different A's (assert, appreciate, apologize, and Adult Voice). In addition, we learned to meet both our needs and other's needs through the five love languages. We also learned three classic signs of a dysfunctional relationship: persecutor, victim, and rescuer. Ultimately, we even learned the balance between transforming relationships that can be redeemed versus terminating those that cannot.

CHAPTER 7

Keeping Your Balance with Growth, Healing, and Maintenance

Now that you have made it this far, we need to start pulling all these skills and concepts together—and keep the balance we have worked so hard to achieve. Earlier in this workbook, we learned that we have not truly and fully changed until we maintain that change over time. Now that we have found some balance, how do we stay balanced?

In this chapter, we will learn two practical exercises that will help you implement all of these skills on a daily basis: the Diary Card and the Pattern Wheel. In addition, you will write yourself a series of letters to help you both process and heal from your previous trauma. Remember the DEAR Adult tools we learned in chapter 6? Soon you will be writing DEAR Self letters to your traumatized self!

Welcome home!

THE DIARY CARD

Now that we have learned all of these great skills, we need a way to make sure we are applying them on a daily basis, starting with the very first skill we learned: mindfulness. The Diary Card is a simple chart that helps you become more mindful of your daily life, while also serving as a reminder to apply your skills.

Remember our magic formula?

applied mindfulness = awareness + acceptance + action

Well, the Diary Card is designed to help you with this process in one single chart. The chart is really easy to use. Simply complete this chart on a daily basis to track your thoughts, feelings, triggers, urges, behaviors, and skills applied. Don't worry about remembering every skill you have learned in this workbook: I have listed them right here for your reference. If you are in counseling with a professional therapist, you might want to bring in your Diary Card to your sessions so that together you can monitor your progress.

Possible Skills

Mindfulness	Self-Care	Sowing SEEDS
SMART Goals	Looking Back	Weeding Myths
Extreme Acceptance	Looking Forward	Fact Checking
Pros and Cons	One Thing at a Time	Acting Opposite
Half Smile	Mini Vacation	Troubleshooting
Change the Temperature	Cheerleading	Adding Positives
Intense Exercise	Journaling	Building Mastery
Controlled Breathing	Enjoyable Activities	Coping Ahead
Muscle Relaxation	Soothing with the Senses	DEAR Adult
Making Comparisons	Ride the Wave	Love Languages
Counting Blessings	Imagery	Other(s):
Finding Humor	Finding Purpose	Other(s):
Container	TEA Party	
Memorization	ANT Stomping	
Helping Others	Working the TOM	

My Diary Card

	Sunday	Monday	Tuesday	Wednesday	Thursday	Friday	Saturday
Thoughts							
Feelings							
Triggers							

	Sunday	Monday	Tuesday	Wednesday	Thursday	Friday	Saturday
Urges							
Behaviors							
Skills							

PATTERN WHEEL

The Diary Card is a great tool to help you remember your skills and to help you monitor your daily ups and downs. But what happens when you're really stuck? What do you do when you find yourself in the same situation over and over again? Or when you keep making the same mistakes time and time again? What happens when you're in a blind spot and you can't see your way out? It's time for the Pattern Wheel!

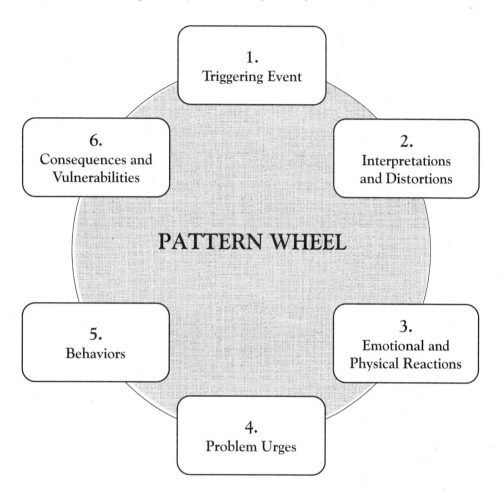

Now let's decode this illustration so you can understand how the Pattern Wheel works.

1. **Triggering event.** First, we identify a problem situation that keeps happening over and over again. This is called the triggering event.

2. **Interpretations and distortions.** Next we need to figure out: What were my beliefs and assumptions about that event? We should identify any ANTs that may be influencing our interpretation.

3. **Emotional and physical reactions.** The next step is to notice our physical and/or emotional reactions to the situation. It is especially helpful if we can figure out where exactly in our body we feel each emotion.

4. **Problem urges.** Next we identify our problem urges. Remember, problem urges are what we feel like doing when triggered, not necessarily what we end up doing. Problem urges, when acted on, make the situation even worse.

5. **Behaviors.** Now we identify our actual behaviors. This is what we end up doing. If we lack self-regulation, our behavior is probably not too different than our problem urge.

6. **Consequences and vulnerabilities.** Finally, we need to identify the consequences of our behaviors. It's especially important to notice when the consequences make us vulnerable (set us up) for the same old prompting event to happen all over again.

But wait, we're not done! Once we have documented steps 1 through 6, we must go back to each step and identify at least one DBT skill that we have learned in this workbook that we can apply to stop the cycle from repeating itself.

Before we look at a sample of the Pattern Wheel in action, there are several things I want you to notice about this exercise. First, did you notice that the Pattern Wheel is designed to increase awareness, just like the Diary Card? While the Diary Card is meant to increase general daily awareness, the Pattern Wheel is designed to increase awareness of specific dysfunctional cycles that trap us. In particular, the Pattern Wheel helps us identify each link in that cycle so that we can develop better insight into what specifically is keeping us stuck.

Second, did you notice that you can break this cycle at any point? There are specific DBT skills that we can use at each link in this chain that will cause the chain to snap. Even though it's always best to break the cycle as soon as possible, it's never too late. You can end the cycle at any time, even if you've spun around this wheel for the hundredth time!

Let's take a look at an example of the Pattern Wheel before you try this on your own. For the sake of argument, let's just pretend that this is not a personal (recurring) example from my own marriage!

1. **Triggering event:** My wife makes a suggestion, perhaps in the form of a helpful critique.

   Possible skills: Mindfulness (awareness + acceptance)

2. **Interpretations and distortions:** "Nothing I ever do is ever good enough for her." Possible ANTs: overgeneralizing, personalizing, mind reading

   Possible skills: Work the TOM, Stomp the ANTs

3. **Emotional and physical reactions:** I feel criticized. I feel humiliated. Breathing increases. Fists start to clench.

   Possible skills: Controlled Breathing, Muscle Relaxation, Self-Soothing

4. **Problem urges:** I feel like criticizing her back.

   Possible skills: Acting Opposite, Ride the Wave, Imagery

5. **Behaviors:** I say something negative to her.

   Possible skills: Finding Humor, Mini Vacation, DEAR Adult—Assert

6. **Consequences and vulnerabilities:** The negative comment I make about my wife confirms her original criticism. Because of how I handled this situation, I have directly contributed toward the same triggering event that started the whole sequence in the first place.

   Possible skills: DEAR Adult—Apologize, Cope Ahead (for next time)

Enough about my own dysfunction. Now it's your turn to practice!

Pattern Wheel Practice

Identify a situation that keeps repeating in your own personal life. Next, identify the domino effect of how one thing leads to another to another, all the way until you are back in the same situation that started off this entire sequence.

1. Triggering Event

What is the situation that keeps happening over and over again?

_____

_____

_____

_____

_____

What skills could I use before this puppy even gets out of the cage?

_____

_____

_____

_____

_____

2. Interpretations and Distortions

What are my beliefs and assumptions about this situation?

_____

_____

_____

_____

_____

Are there any ANTs influencing my interpretation?

_____

_____

_____

_____

_____

What skills could I use to come up with a more accurate interpretation?

_____

_____

_____

_____

_____

3. Physical and Emotional Reactions

What am I feeling physically in response to this situation?

_____

_____

_____

_____

_____

What am I feeling emotionally in response to this situation?

_____

_____

_____

_____

_____

Try to identify a specific connection between each physical feeling and each emotional feeling.

_____

_____

_____

_____

_____

What skills could I use to cope with these feelings?

_____

_____

_____

_____

_____

4. Problem Urges

What do I feel like doing in this situation?

_____

_____

_____

_____

_____

Would this reaction help the situation or make it worse?

_____

_____

_____

_____

_____

What skills could I use to cope with these urges?

_____

_____

_____

_____

_____

5. Behaviors

How do I usually handle this situation?

_____

_____

_____

_____

_____

What skills could I use to handle this situation differently in the future?

_____

_____

_____

_____

_____

6. Consequences and Vulnerabilities

What are the real-world consequences of my behavior?

_____

_____

_____

_____

_____

How does my behavior contribute toward the same situation that started off this whole ordeal?

_____

_____

_____

_____

_____

What skills can I use to repair the damage and prevent another go-around?

_____

_____

_____

_____

_____

DEAR SELF

In the chapter on Restoring Balance with Relationships, do you remember how we learned the DEAR Adult tool to assert, appreciate, and apologize? In this chapter, you are going to learn a similar tool to continue your healing journey: DEAR Self.

You will be writing a series of letters to your traumatized self. Please note: The following exercises should be completed only (1) if you are currently receiving support from a professional counselor or (2) if you have already worked your way through the rest of this workbook. Here's why: There are many models for treating trauma, but they all overlap on one point: Your life should not currently be in active crisis when you process a trauma memory. For example, you should not be super depressed, you should not be in the midst of a hard-core addiction, you should not be in an unsafe environment, and you should certainly not be suicidal. In other words, all trauma models say that you need to reach a safe level of stability—including self-regulation—before processing memories that will be inherently triggering. And that's precisely why I have included this exercise in the final chapter. By now you have leaned the skills you need to deal with triggers!

Think of one of your traumatic experiences. If this is your first time doing this, do not select the worst trauma that ever happened to you. Instead, choose one to practice with that is not so triggering that it will cause you to relapse in your treatment. The format you will be using to write this letter is DEAR Self.

D—Describe. In the first part of your DEAR Self letter, you will *describe* a traumatic event that happened to you. You will retell the specific order of events. You will also describe what you experienced with each of your five senses (or as many as apply): what you saw, what you heard, what you smelled, what you tasted, and what you felt.

E—Express and Empathize. *Express* all the emotions that you felt when the trauma happened, as well as the emotions you experienced after the trauma ended. If necessary, identify the emotions that became frozen, numb, or stuck as a result of the trauma. In addition, since you are writing this letter to your traumatized self, provide the *empathy* that you never received at the time.

A—Assert, Appreciate, Apologize. First, you will *assert* to your traumatized self that what happened was wrong and was not your fault, no matter what someone has told you. You may need to identify any ANTs that you still believe about the trauma, and then dispute those ANTs with balanced thinking. Second, you will verbalize *appreciation* to your traumatized self for how strong and brave you are to have survived this trauma. Be sure to elaborate on all of your positive qualities that allowed you to survive the trauma. Third, you will write the *apology* that you never received or that you wish you could have received. You are not apologizing for your own trauma. Rather, you are apologizing that the trauma happened in the first place.

R—Reinforce. *Reinforce* means to strengthen something or to increase a behavior. In this case, you are going to strengthen your relationship to yourself as well as increase your dedication to the healing process through many R words: remind, reassure, recall, recommit, reflect, redeem, repurpose, redefine, and re-envision. You will *remind* yourself that the trauma is now over; you will *reassure* yourself that you are now safe. You will *recall* all the skills you have learned along the way—and you will *recommit* to practicing these skills for as long as it takes.

You will also *reflect* on what you have learned from the trauma, and even find ways to *redeem* or *repurpose* your suffering. Ask yourself questions such as: *How can my trauma be transformed into something positive? Or to help others? What insights have I learned from this trauma that I could not have learned otherwise? How can I use my trauma to help transform myself, others, and the world?*

A final way to reinforce both yourself and your healing journey is to *redefine* your goals, plans, and dreams moving forward. What future can you *re-envision* that is no longer defined by your trauma? What is your plan to live, love, and laugh as you never have before?

Self. Do you recall from the chapter on relationships how important your delivery is? Well I can't think of any other letter in which your delivery will be more important! Remember that you are writing each part of this letter to your traumatized self. Therefore, remember to be kind, gentle, and compassionate—the same way you would write to your best friend. In addition, remember to use all of the skills you have learned so far in this book. It is especially important to remember to be accepting and nonjudgmental toward yourself.

My DEAR Self Outline and Letter

As you did with DEAR Adult for assert, appreciate, and apologize, you will begin DEAR Self with an outline. After you complete the outline, please write out your letter to yourself. If at any point writing this letter becomes too triggering, stop this exercise and take care of yourself by using your skills!

D—Describe the traumatic event in as much detail as I remember, including as many of the five senses that apply.

_____

_____

_____

_____

_____

_____

_____

_____

_____

_____

_____

_____

_____

_____

_____

E—Express the emotions I felt both at the time of the trauma and afterward.

_____

_____

_____

_____

_____

_____

_____

_____

_____

Identify any emotions that became frozen, numb, or stuck as a result of the trauma.

_____

_____

_____

_____

_____

_____

_____

_____

_____

Provide the empathy I never received.

_____
_____
_____
_____
_____
_____
_____
_____
_____

A—Assert that the trauma was not my fault.

_____
_____
_____
_____
_____
_____
_____
_____
_____
_____
_____

Identify any ANTs that I still believe about the trauma. Dispute those ANTs with balanced thinking.

_____

_____

_____

_____

_____

_____

_____

_____

_____

_____

Appreciate how strong and brave I was to survive this trauma.

_____

_____

_____

_____

_____

_____

_____

_____

_____

_____

Apologize to myself vicariously. Provide the apology I never received or wish I could have received.

_____
_____
_____
_____
_____
_____
_____
_____
_____

R—Reinforce my healing journey.

_____
_____
_____
_____
_____
_____
_____
_____
_____
_____
_____

Remind myself that the trauma is over.

_____

_____

_____

_____

_____

_____

_____

_____

_____

Reassure myself that I am now safe.

_____

_____

_____

_____

_____

_____

_____

_____

_____

_____

Recall all the skills I have learned, and recommit to practicing these skills for as long as it takes.

_____
_____
_____
_____
_____
_____
_____
_____
_____
_____

Let's continue to reflect. What insights have I learned from this trauma?

_____
_____
_____
_____
_____
_____
_____
_____
_____

How can my trauma be redeemed or repurposed for good?

_____

_____

_____

_____

_____

_____

_____

_____

_____

How can I use my trauma to help transform myself, others, and the world?

_____

_____

_____

_____

_____

_____

_____

_____

_____

_____

What future can I re-envision for myself that is no longer defined by my trauma?

_____

_____

_____

_____

_____

_____

_____

_____

_____

_____

How can I redefine my new goals, plans, and dreams moving forward?

_____

_____

_____

_____

_____

_____

_____

_____

_____

_____

_____

Self—Be sure to speak to yourself in a gentle, compassionate tone, the same way you would talk to your best friend. And don't forget to apply as much self-care as you need as you write your letter!

Once you have completed your DEAR Self outline, you can write your letter. When your letter is finished, show it to someone you know and trust. Complete as many of these DEAR Self letters as necessary to process and heal from your traumas. Here is space to get you started.

_____

_____

_____

_____

_____

_____

_____

_____

_____

_____

_____

_____

_____

_____

_____

_____

_____

_____

_____

THE LAST, LAST WORD

In this final chapter, you have learned to integrate—and maintain—all of the skills you have learned throughout this entire workbook. First, you learned how to keep a Diary Card, which will help you monitor your thoughts, feelings, triggers, urges, behaviors, and skills on a daily basis. Second, you learned to complete a Pattern Wheel, which will help you figure out which skills you need to apply in order to get out of any ruts that you might still find yourself in. And finally, you learned to write DEAR Self letters to process, integrate, and heal from your trauma.

As I mentioned at the beginning, you may have completed this entire workbook and find that you still have some symptoms of PTSD. That does not mean that DBT did not work or that you did not do this workbook right. On the contrary, what that might mean is that you need to consult with a professional counselor, preferably one who is trained in trauma work. A professional counselor might help you develop your DBT skills even further or use a different model altogether. Either option is fine. In fact, DBT skills often lay the groundwork for deeper trauma work with other models.

~~~~~

In ancient Greece, in the temple where oracles from the gods were supposedly received, there were two inscriptions on the wall: "Know thyself" and "Moderation in all things." Apparently, no matter what the question or problem was, the answer included some combination of self-awareness and balance! These two maxims summarize the key themes of this entire book. Thousands of years later, is it possible that mindfulness and balance are still the keys to many if not most of life's problems, including healing from trauma? Now that you have completed this workbook, you'll go forward with "prophetic" wisdom!

Acknowledgments

Primeramente, gracias a mi hermosa y paciente esposa por aguantar todos mis proyectos locos.

In addition, thanks to Sheresa Wilson-DeVries, PAC, for her constant moral, logistical, and literary support.

References

Alcoholics Anonymous. 2002. *Twelve Steps and Twelve Traditions.* New York: Alcoholics Anonymous World Services.

American Psychiatric Association. 2013. *Diagnostic and Statistical Manual of Mental Disorders.* 5th ed. Washington, DC: APA.

Avraham, Y., M. Mikulincer, C. Nardi, and S. Shoham. 1992. "The Use of Individual Goal-Setting and Ongoing Evaluation in the Treatment of Combat-Related Chronic PTSD." *Journal of Traumatic Stress* 5(2): 195–204.

Beck, J. S. 2011. *Cognitive Behavior Therapy: Basics and Beyond.* 2nd ed. New York: Guilford Press.

Berk-Clark, C. V. D., S. Secrest, J. Walls, et al. 2018. "Association Between Posttraumatic Stress Disorder and Lack of Exercise, Poor Diet, Obesity, and Co-Occuring Smoking: A Systematic Review and Meta-Analysis." *Health Psychology* 37(5): 407–416.

Berne, E. 2015. *Transactional Analysis in Psychotherapy: A Systematic Individual and Social Psychiatry.* Eastfort, CT: Martino Fine Books. (Original work published 1961.)

Bowen, S., and A. Marlatt. 2008. "Surfing the Urge: Brief Mindfulness-Based Intervention for College Student Smokers." *Psychology of Addictive Behaviors* 23(4): 666–671.

Buunk, A., P. Buunk, R. Zurriaga, and P. González. 2006. "Social Comparison, Coping and Depression in People with Spinal Cord Injury." *Psychology & Health* 21(6): 791–807. https://doi.org/10.1080/14768320500444117.

Carey, B. 2011. "Expert on Mental Illness Reveals Her Own Fight." *The New York Times,* June 23, A1.

Casiday, R. 2015. "Volunteering and Health: What Impact Does It Really Have?" October 30. Available from: https://www.researchgate.net/publication/228628782_Volunteering_and_Health_What_Impact_Does_It_Really_Have. Accessed July 13, 2018.

Castillo-Pérez, S., V. Gómez-Pérez, M. C. Velasco, E. Pérez-Campos, and M. A. Mayoral. 2010. "Effects of Music Therapy on Depression Compared with Psychotherapy." *The Arts in Psychotherapy* 37(5): 387–390.

Chapman, G. 2015. *The Five Love Languages: The Secret to Love That Lasts.* Chicago: Northfield Publishing.

Connors, G. J., C. C. DiClemente, M. M. Velasquez, and D. M. Donovan. 2015. *Substance Abuse Treatment and the Stages of Change: Selecting and Planning Interventions.* 2nd ed. New York: Guilford Press.

Contractor, A. A., C. Armour, D. Forbes, and J. D. Elhai. 2016. "Posttraumatic Stress Disorder's Underlying Dimensions and Their Relation with Impulsivity Facets." *Journal of Nervous and Mental Disorders* 204(1): 20–25.

Curran, L. 2016. *The Adverse Childhood Experiences Study.* PESI: Master Clinician Series.

Davies, S. 2014. *Johari's Window.* Bristol, UK: SilverWood Books.

Duenwalk, M. 2005. "The Physiology of Facial Expressions: A Self-Conscious Look of Fear, Anger, or Happiness Can Reveal More Than a Lie Detector." *Discover,* January 2.

Essa, R. M., N. I. A. A. Ismail, N. I. Hassan. 2017. "Effect of Progressive Muscle Relaxation Technique on Stress, Anxiety, and Depression After Hysterectomy." *Journal of Nursing Education and Practice* 7(7): 77–86.

Field, T., M. Hernandez-Reif, M. Diego, S. Schanberg, and C. Kuhn. 2005. "Cortisol Decreases and Serotonin and Dopamine Increase Following Massage Therapy." *International Journal of Neuroscience* 115(10): 1397–1413.

Figley, C. R. 2002. "Compassion Fatigue: Psychotherapists' Chronic Lack of Self-Care." *Journal of Clinical Psychology* 58: 1433–1441.

Fowler, J. C., J. G. Allen, J. M. Oldhamab, and C. Frueh. 2013. "Exposure to Interpersonal Trauma, Attachment Insecurity, and Depression Severity." *Journal of Affective Disorders* 149(1–3): 313–318.

Frank, Mark G. 2016. *Understanding Non-Verbal Communication.* Chantilly, VA: The Teaching Company.

Frankl, V. E. 1984. *Man's Search for Meaning: An Introduction to Logotherapy.* New York: Simon & Schuster.

Gilman, R., J. A. Schumm, and K. M. Chard. 2012. "Hope as a Change Mechanism in the Treatment of Posttraumatic Stress Disorder." *Psychological Trauma: Theory, Research, Practice, and Policy* 4(3): 270–277.

Godley, S. H., and J. E. Smith. 2016. *The Adolescent Community Reinforcement Approach: A Clinical Guide for Treating Substance Use Disorders.* Normal, IL: Chestnut Health Systems.

Horne-Thompson, A., and D. Grocke. 2008. "The Effect of Music Therapy on Anxiety in Patients Who Are Terminally Ill." *Journal of Palliative Medicine* 11: 582–590.

Hutchinson, S. L., D. P. Loy, D. A. Kleiber, and J. Dattilo. 2003. "Leisure as a Coping Resource: Variations in Coping with Traumatic Injury and Illness." *Leisure Sciences* 25: 2–3, 143–161.

Kearney, D. J., K. McDermott, C. Malte, M. Martinez, and T. L. Simpson. 2011. "Association of Participation in a Mindfulness Program with Measures of PTSD, Depression, and Quality of Life in a Veteran Sample." *Journal of Clinical Psychology* 68: 1–16.

Kehoe, D. 2014. *Effective Communication Skills.* Chantilly, VA: The Teaching Company.

Kimiaee, S. A., H. Khademian, and H. Farhadi. 2012. "Quran Memorization and Its Effects on the Elements of Mental Health." *Journal of Woman and Society* 2(4): 1–20.

Kübler-Ross, E., and D. Kessler. 2014. *On Grief and Grieving: Finding the Meaning of Grief Through the Five Stages of Loss.* New York: Scribner.

Lemon, K. 2004. "An Assessment of Treating Depression and Anxiety with Aromatherapy." *International Journal of Aromatherapy* 14(2): 63–69.

Linehan, M. M. 2015. *DBT® Skills Training Manual.* 2nd ed. New York: Guilford Press.

Lynn, W. M. 2011. "MegaTips 2: Twenty Tested Techniques to Increase Your Tips." *Cornell Hospitality Tools* 2(1): 6–21.

Maslow, A. H. 2013. *A Theory of Human Motivation.* Eastfort, CT: Martino Fine Books.

Matthieu, M. M., K. A. Lawrence, and E. Robertson-Blackmore. 2017. "The Impact of a Civic Service Program on Biopsychosocial Outcomes of Post 9/11 U.S. Military Veterans." *Psychiatry Research* 248: 111–116.

Neacsiu, A. D., M. Bohus, and M. M. Linehan. 2015. "Dialectical Behavior Therapy Skills: An Intervention for Emotion Dysregulation." *Research Gate*, January.

Ostafin, B. D., and G. A. Marlatt. 2008. "Surfing the Urge: Experiential Acceptance Moderates the Relation Between Automatic Alcohol Motivation and Hazardous Drinking." *Journal of Social and Clinical Psychology* 27(4): 404–418.

Parncutt, R. 2016. "Prenatal Development." In G. E. McPherson (ed.), *The Child as Musician: A Handbook of Musical Development* (1–31). Oxford, UK: Oxford University Press.

Peck, M. S. 1978. *The Road Less Traveled: A New Psychology of Love, Traditional Values, and Spiritual Growth.* New York: Simon and Schuster.

Pressman, S. D., K. A. Matthews, S. Cohen, L. M. Martire, M. Scheier, A. Baum, and R. Schulz. 2009. "Association of Enjoyable Leisure Activities with Psychological and Physical Well-Being." *Psychosomatic Medicine* 71(7): 725–732.

Rosenbaum, S., C. Sherrington, and A. Tiedemann. 2015. "Exercise Augmentation Compared with Usual Care for Post-Traumatic Stress Disorder: A Randomized Controlled Trial." *Acta Psychiatrica Scandinavica* 131(5): 350–359.

Sayer, N. A., S. Noorbaloochi, P. A. Frazie, J. W. Pennebaker, R. J. Orazem, P. P. Schnurr, M. Murdoch, K. F. Carlson, A. Gravely, and B. T. Litz. 2015. "Randomized Controlled Trial of Online Expressive Writing to Address Readjustment Difficulties Among U.S. Afghanistan and Iraq War Veterans." *Journal of Traumatic Stress* 28(5): 381–390.

Scott, S. J. 2017. *S.M.A.R.T. Goals Made Simple—10 Steps to Master Your Personal and Career Goals.* Cranberry, NJ: Old Town Publishing LLC.

Seppälä, E. M., J. B. Nitschke, D. L. Tudorascu, A. Hayes, M. R. Goldstein, D. T. Nguyen, D. Perlman, and R. J. Davidson. 2014. "Breathing-Based Meditation Decreases Posttraumatic Stress Disorder Symptoms in U.S. Military Veterans: A Randomized Controlled Longitudinal Study." *Journal of Traumatic Stress* 27(4): 397–405.

Shoda, Y., and S. LeeTiernan. 2002. "What Remains Invariant?: Finding Order Within a Person's Thoughts, Feelings, and Behaviors Across Situations." In *Advances in Personality Science* (241–270), edited by D. Cervone and W. Mischel. New York: Guilford Press.

Siegel, D. J. 2007. *The Mindful Brain: Reflection and Attunement in the Cultivation of Well-Being.* New York: W. W. Norton.

Siegel, R. D. 2014. *The Science of Mindfulness: A Research-Based Path to Well-Being.* Chantilly, VA: The Teaching Company.

Sliter, M., A. Kale, and Z. Yuan. 2014. "Is Humor the Best Medicine? The Buffering Effect of Coping Humor on Traumatic Stressors in Firefighters." *Journal of Organizational Behavior* 35(2): 257–272.

Tusek, D., J. M. Church, and V. W. Fazio. 2006. "Guided Imagery as a Coping Strategy for Perioperative Patients." *AORN Journal,* August 29. https://doi.org/10.1016/S0001–2092(06)62917–7.

Van der Kolk, B. A. 2014. *The Body Keeps the Score: Brain, Mind, and Body in the Healing of Trauma.* New York: Viking.

Van Raalte, J. L., B. W. Brewer, B. P. Lewis, D. E. Linder, G. Wildman, and J. Kozimer. 1995. "Cork! The Effects of Positive and Negative Self-Talk on Dart Throwing Performance." *Journal of Sport Behavior* 18(1): 50–57.

Vernon, L. L., J. M. Dillon, and R. W. Steiner. 2009. "Proactive Coping, Gratitude, and Posttraumatic Stress Disorder in College Women." *Anxiety, Stress & Coping* 22(1): 117–127.

Vess, M. 2012. "Warm Thoughts: Attachment Anxiety and Sensitivity to Temperature Cues." *Psychological Science* 23(5): 472–474.

Watt, L. M., and P. Cappeliez. 2000. "Integrative and Instrumental Reminiscence Therapies for Depression in Older Adults: Intervention Strategies and Treatment Effectiveness." *Aging & Mental Health* 4(2): 166–177. https://doi.org/10.1080/13607860050008691.

Weinhold, B. K., and J. B. Weinhold. 2014. *How to Break Free of the Drama Triangle and Victim Consciousness.* Asheville, NC: CICRCL Press.

Kirby Reutter, PhD, is a bilingual licensed psychologist, licensed mental health counselor, and internationally certified substance abuse counselor. Reutter has widely presented his unique approaches to psychotherapy throughout the nation, including one TEDx talk and three trainings for the US military. In addition, Reutter has conducted international research on spiritual coping, the results of which have been published by three different sources and personally presented at the Massachusetts Institute of Technology in 2015. Reutter was named a New England Scholar in 2002, as well as Northcentral University's Alumni of the Year in 2018 for his work with trauma treatment, including survivors of human trafficking. Reutter currently contracts with the US Department of Homeland Security.

Foreword writer **Dawn DePasquale, LMHC**, is a national speaker, trainer, and media presence for mental health issues. She is also founder, CEO, and clinical director of Bell Mental Health Associates, LLC. She spends her free time writing and illustrating her first two therapeutic children's book series, *The Ninja Therapist* and *The Dragon Worriers*, and writes for the SouthCoast Media Group's online advice blog, "Ask Dawn."

Real change *is* possible

For more than forty-five years, New Harbinger has published proven-effective self-help books and pioneering workbooks to help readers of all ages and backgrounds improve mental health and well-being, and achieve lasting personal growth. In addition, our spirituality books offer profound guidance for deepening awareness and cultivating healing, self-discovery, and fulfillment.

Founded by psychologist Matthew McKay and Patrick Fanning, New Harbinger is proud to be an independent, employee-owned company. Our books reflect our core values of integrity, innovation, commitment, sustainability, compassion, and trust. Written by leaders in the field and recommended by therapists worldwide, New Harbinger books are practical, accessible, and provide real tools for real change.

 newharbingerpublications